ANGELS ON ASSIGNMENT AGAIN

DEFENDER
CRANE, MO

ANGELS ON ASSIGNMENT AGAIN: God's Real-Life Guardians of Saints at Work in the World Today
By Jennifer LeClaire

Printed in the United States of America

Scripture taken from the King James Version unless otherwise noted.

Cover design by Jeffrey Mardis
ISBN-978-0998142685

Dedication

I dedicate this book to all those who are on a genuine pursuit of the truth regarding angels on assignment; to all those who are committed to avoiding extreme teachings on angels that can lead people into deception in the last days; and to every believer who has been encountered by angels but did not have the language or Scripture to understand or explain what they experienced.

Contents

Acknowledgments

I'm grateful to the Lord for opening my eyes to the reality of angels on assignment in my life. I appreciate Tom Horn reaching out to me about revisiting the classic book, *Angels on Assignment*, including exploring the controversy it created. I appreciate his willingness to dive into topics that many Christians ponder but would otherwise not have the time to study.

Introduction

For many years, I neglected the study of angels on assignment. Although I knew at times that angels had intervened on my behalf—there was the time my car spun out of control and I cried out "Jesus" in a loud voice and some unseen force instantly stabilized the car in the midst of a violent rain storm—angelology was not on my radar screen in the early years of my walk with Christ.

Perhaps if I had seen an angel with my own two eyes as my friend did on a camping trip in the mountains of North Carolina, I would have pressed into the reality of angels on assignment.

I'll never forget the scene: We hiked up the Smoky Mountains far higher than my friend had told me we were headed. When we arrived, I was absolutely exhausted and wanted nothing more than to lie down and sleep. Of course, we had to set up the tent first. Since I knew nothing about setting up tents, I assisted as best I could while my friend did most of the work. Of course, I figured, it served her right since she had told me we were hiking a mile up the mountain and it was surely ten miles or more by this point.

After the tent was set up and the fire was going, she informed me we had to do one more thing before we settled in for the night—we had to hang the bag of food we carried up the mountain on the bear pole. Yes…I said "bear pole." She explained with intensity that if we left the food out in the camp, hungry bears might invade the site and devour us along with the trail mix.

My friend climbed up the bear pole and hung the food at its top, and we finally closed the zipper on the tent. The nightmare of my day was over. When the sun rose, I felt like I had been in the wilderness for forty days like Jesus. After that stretch of time, the Bible says He was hungry (Luke 4:2). I was not only hungry—I was *starving*. I was going after that trail mix with a vengeance. Or at least I tried to. I couldn't get it down from the bear pole.

I woke up my friend and politely suggested that she shimmy up the pole and retrieve said trail mix. She shimmied alright, but the knot she tied in the rope was so tight that she couldn't loosen it. She hemmed and hawed while I just about went into travail. My flesh was crying out to the living God for sustenance, and it was looking like we would die on that mountain from starvation.

Long story short, my friend got hold of a camping knife and set out to cut the knot and set the trail mix free. It was a brilliant idea that was poorly executed. Instead of cutting the knot, she cut the bag. Trail mix went flying everywhere. In that moment, all I could think about was the bears coming into our camp that night seeking whom they may devour. Since I had more fat on my body than she did, I was sure they would devour me first.

When night fell again, I was hungry, sore, tired, and scared. Not to mention *cold*. It was freezing up in those mountains! I closed the zipper on the tent and lay my head on the pillow in complete darkness—there was no moonlight and not a star in the sky. The only available light was the flickering flames on the fire in the center of our camp. I wondered for a moment if we had descended into hell.

Determined to make the best of it, I bundled myself up as tightly as I could and started counting sheep in my head. I heard the rustling noise that I was sure originated from a bear outside the tent. I was certain it was a grizzly scavenging for the M&Ms and nuts that were scattered to and fro. I am not sure why, but I unzipped the tent door and poked my head outside. I don't know what I thought I would do if I saw a bear. I guess the fasting had gone to my head.

What I saw was something darker than the blackest shade of black lunge toward me with vicious force. It scared me half to death…and I screamed. My body flew to the back of the tent. Then I froze. Speechless. Finally, I managed to utter one word…

"Bear…"

My friend didn't believe me. She decided to take a look for herself. I feared for her life, but was still frozen like an ice sculpture, so I watched in silent terror as she looked out the tent doors. I was sure she had sealed her fate.

She stuck her head out for what seemed like an eternity when suddenly I heard her exclaim, "Wow! Wow! Wow!"

Somewhat annoyed, I said, "What?"

Her only response: "Wow!"

Especially annoyed at this point, I replied, "What?!"

She then informed me that there were giant angels, one on either side of the tent, with swords drawn. They were protecting us. They were angels of protection. God had opened her eyes and allowed her to see in the spirit realm. What I had seen, I later learned, was a spirit of fear. I felt like I got the short end of that supernatural stick. After all, it was her fault that we needed angelic protection from bears and fear demons in the first place!

Over the years, I've come to understand that angels are all around us. There are more angels than there are demons—only one-third of the angels followed Lucifer in his insurrection. The angels are innumerable (Hebrews 12:22). Angels accomplish many different tasks as part of their ministry to the heirs of salvation—and they excel in strength to do God's will (Psalm 103:20).

Angels are more active in our lives—and in the world—than we can imagine. Indeed, if we only knew. And angelic activity is increasing.

When Roland Buck told Charles and Frances Hunter about his angelic encounters as related in the classic book, *Angels on Assignment*, his stories fascinated a generation. This book you hold in your hands doesn't pretend to be a sequel to that book. Rather, it's a fresh look at the reality that angels are on assignment. I didn't ignore the evidence of angelic encounters—no matter how bizarre they seemed—in my research. Neither did I ignore the troubling controversies, past or present, in the realm of angelic visitations.

I pray this book stirs curiosity, answers questions, and sends you on your own path to studying what the Bible says about spirits sent to minister to the heirs of salvation (Hebrews 1:14).

I

What People Believe about Angels

Some people all-out refuse to believe in God, heaven, hell, the devil—or angels. Of course, that doesn't negate the reality of the spirit realm or the Creator of the Universe.

The Holy Spirit, the author of Scripture, saw fit to record hundreds of manifestations and encounters with angels. In fact, angels are mentioned 108 times in the Old Testament and 165 times in the New Testament. That's a lot, considering there are only sixty-six books in the Bible. In fact, if you average out those numbers, you come to a clear conclusion: Angels are mentioned or seen working over four times for every book included in the canon of Scripture. I am sure the world could not contain all the books that could be written about angelic activity any more than it could contain all the books recounting the works of Christ while He walked the earth (see John 21:25).

Angels are not omnipresent—only God is omnipresent. But angels are everywhere. All day, every day—and all night every night—angels are on assignment. In every nation of the earth, angels are among the agents executing God's will in the earth. If we could pull back the veil separating the natural world from the spiritual world, we would doubtless see innumerable angels all around us.

Isaiah tells us of the seraphim, a class of angels that has six wings (see Isaiah 6:2). Jude tells us of angels who overrode their authority and are kept in eternal chains in darkness until Judgement Day (see Jude 1:6). Acts describes an angel giving Philip an instruction to go to a desert place for ministry (see Acts 8:26). And the list goes on—and on and on.

I've never seen an angel, but I've never seen God, either, and I am utterly convinced He exists. When it comes to angels, we must not be like doubting Thomas when so much evidence—biblical and experiential—proves angels exist. Thomas, one of Jesus' original disciples, vowed he would not believe Jesus was risen from the dead unless he saw Him and put his finger in the nail prints and put his hand in His side (see John 20:25).

> *After eight days His disciples were again inside with the doors shut, and Thomas was with them. Jesus came and stood among them, and said, "Peace be with you." Then He said to Thomas, "Put your finger here, and look at My hands. Put your hand here and place it in My side. Do not be faithless, but believing."*
>
> *Thomas answered Him, "My Lord and my God!"*
>
> *Jesus said to him, "Thomas, because you have seen Me, you have believed. Blessed are those who have not seen, and have yet believed."*
>
> JOHN 20:26–29

I believe in the reality of the Father, the Son, the Holy Spirit, heaven, hell, angels, and demons. I can sense the presence of God, His holy angels, and incorrigible demons that come to kill, steal and destroy (see John 10:10). I walk by faith in the Word of God and not by sight (see 2 Corinthians 5:7)—I walk by discernment, by the leading of the Holy Spirit (see Romans 8:14). So should you.

An increasing number of people—ministry leaders and everyday Joes—are reporting angelic visitations, activities, and other manifestations that line up with Scripture. Although there are some who are likely puffed up in the imagination of their mind, reporting things they have not seen just to get attention (see Colossians 2:18), I believe the majority of these reports are bona fide. Scientists point to coping mechanisms or fantasies, but God is not a man that He should lie, nor the son of man that He should repent (see Numbers 23:19). Angels have been part of God's plan for thousands of years, and these heavenly beings are still on assignment today.

MOST AMERICANS BELIEVE IN THE REALITY OF ANGELS

Whether or not they call themselves Christians, most Americans believe in the reality of angels. A 2011 Associated Press-GfK poll[1] revealed that 77 percent of adults have faith that these supernatural beings are for real. That said, religion influences that faith.

Breaking the data down, 88 percent of the overall Christian population believes in angels. Ninety-five percent of evangelical Christians believe in angels, as do 94 percent of people who attend religious services weekly. Most of non-Christians also believe in the heavenly beings, along with more than 40 percent of those who never go to church. Demographics-wise, women are more likely than men to believe angels exist, as are people over age 30 compared to younger adults.

With so many tragic events in the world today—including natural disasters and terror attacks—still only 56 percent of Americans believe in a literal devil, according to a True Life in God Foundation Poll.[2] Even fewer believe in a literal hell (53 percent) and fewer still (43 percent) believe in hell as "a place of suffering and punishment where people go after they die." And only 41 percent identify the devil as "Satan the fallen angel who rebelled against God and now tempts humans to do the same."

"The devil's most powerful tool is convincing us that he—and hell—do not exist," says Vassula Ryden, an international author/humanitarian who commissioned the study. "He works subtly and silently, feeding our doubts and inadequacies, sowing dissension and creating chaos and confusion in our lives. Evil is real, and we have to know how to respond to it."

According to the Association of Religion Data Archives, 60 percent of those surveyed in 2007 believe in angels; 21 percent said angels "probably" exist; 10 percent said "probably not;" and 9 percent said absolutely not.[3] On the flip side—or should I say dark side—45 percent believe in demons; 22 percent say demons "probably exist." And 19.5 percent argue they probably do not exist, and 13 percent say demons absolutely do not exist.[4]

A 2016 Gallup poll survey reveals that 89 percent of Americans believe in God, 61 percent believe in the devil, 71 percent believe in heaven, 64 percent believe in hell, and 72 percent believe in angels. And a Pew Research U.S. Religious Landscape Survey reveals that nearly seven in ten Americans (68 percent) believe that angels and demons are active in the world.[5]

Belief in Guardian Angels Goes Mainstream in America

Fifty-five percent of Americans believe a guardian angel has protected them from harm. That's according to Baylor Institute for Religious Studies' *What Americans Really Believe.*[6] That stunned researcher Dr. Christopher Bader.

"That was something that was a complete surprise because this is not a question, do you believe in guardian angels or do you believe in angels," Bader says. "This is a very specific question: Do you believe you have been protected from harm by a guardian angel? Do you believe you avoided an accident through the agency of a guardian angel? To find out that more than half of the American public believes this was shocking to me. I did not expect that."

Believers and unbelievers alike seem familiar with the promise of Psalm 91:11–12—the promise of guardian angels: "He shall give His angels charge over you to guard you in all your ways. They shall bear you up in their hands, lest you strike your foot against a stone." But that's not the only Scripture that reveals the reality of angels on assignment to guard. Let's look at a few others:

The Lord told Moses:

> *Indeed, I am going to send an angel before you to guard you along the way and to bring you into the place which I have prepared.*
>
> EXODUS 23:20

Jesus supports the truth that angels are still on this assignment in the New Testament:

> *See that you do not despise one of these little ones. For I say to you that in heaven their angels always see the face of My Father who is in heaven.*
>
> MATTHEW 18:10

Notice the word "angels" there is plural, signifying that we have more than one angel assigned to us.

The writer of Hebrews reports:

> *But to which of the angels did He at any time say, "Sit at My right hand, until I make Your enemies Your footstool"? Are they not all ministering spirits sent out to minister to those who will inherit salvation?*
>
> HEBREWS 1:13–14

Clearly, there are angels assigned to guard us. But what is a guardian angel? The simplest definition is "an angel who guards." Guardian angels provide protection from danger. Many unbelievers point to guardian angels in the face of deliverance from evil. Consider these reports from ABC News:[7]

> Stephanie Schwabe, 54, of Charleston, S.C., was cave diving for a research project in the Bahamas when she lost her safety line. "I suddenly realized I was in trouble," she said. "My heart rate, I could hear it bouncing in my eyes, and I just kind of sat down on the [cave] floor and cried." Schwabe's husband and diving partner, Rob Palmer, had died in a diving accident in the Red Sea only weeks before. Now, alone, she was facing her own dark death. "Suddenly, the whole cave brightened up," she said. Schwabe said that into that watery world floated the words of her late husband: "Believe you can, believe you can't; either way, you are right." "And then I calmed down and then I suddenly looked around and I saw what I thought was a white thread," she said. "It was kind of like he was there for me, in a way—in an emotional way… Only my guardian angel could have saved me from such an accident."

In another account, Rose Benvenuto, a 71-year-old woman from Poughquag, New York, is convinced she saw her guardian angel at the scene of a horrible car accident that could have killed her—and she says she has a photograph that proves it. That photo went viral online, and Benvenuto argues, "Only my guardian angel could have saved me from such an accident."[8]

According to one study,[9] belief in guardian angels actually makes people more cautious rather than more reckless. This is wisdom, considering the account of one of Christ's three recorded tests during His forty days in the wilderness:

Then the devil took Him up into the holy city, and set Him on the highest point of the temple, and said to Him, "If You are the Son of God, throw Yourself down. For it is written, 'He shall give His angels charge concerning you,' and 'In their hands they shall lift you up, lest at any time you dash your foot against a stone.'" Jesus said to him, "It is also written, 'You shall not tempt the Lord your God.'"

LUKE 4:5–7

Researchers David Etkin, Jelena Ivanova, Susan MacGregor, and Alalia Spektor surveyed 198 people in the SAGE study. Of those who believe in guardian angels, 68 percent said that this belief affects how they take risks.[10] In other words, though some might take more risks in reliance on guardian angels, the overwhelming majority are more risk-averse than their non-believing counterparts.

When asked to provide their opinion about risky driving, for example, the majority of those in the SAGE study who do not believe in guardian angels felt that driving twenty kilometers per hour over the speed limit was a risk level of two on a scale of one to five, while the majority of those who do believe in guardian angels believed that it was a risk level of three.[11] The researchers' conclusion: "It may be that people who have a tendency to view the world as being risky or potentially dangerous are more inclined to have a belief in personal guardian spirits."

WHAT VARIOUS RELIGIONS AND ETHNICITIES BELIEVE ABOUT ANGELS

Many religions believe in angels, but what they believe about angels varies widely. According to Pew Research,[12] majorities of Jehovah's Witnesses (78 percent), members of evangelical (61 percent) and historically black (59 percent) Protestant churches, and Mormons (59 percent) are completely convinced of the existence of angels and demons. In stark contrast, Pew reports, majorities of Jews (73 percent), Buddhists (56 percent), Hindus (55 percent) and the unaffiliated (54 percent) do not believe that angels and demons are active in the world. Let's take a look at what various religions and ethnicities believe about angels.

Christianity: The crux of a Christian's understanding of angels on a personal level is found in Hebrews 1:14:

> *Are they not all ministering spirits sent out to minister to those who will inherit salvation?*

Angels serve as messengers in the New Testament much of the time, but they are also seen in a deliverance function. An angel appeared to Zacharias to tell him he would have a son named John (Luke 1:11–12). An angel appeared to Mary to tell her she was carrying the Messiah (Luke 1:26–28, 30–31). Angels ministered to Jesus in the wilderness (Luke 4). An angel set the apostles free from prison (Acts 5:17–20). And an angel visited Paul to let him know the passengers on a ship that carried him would not lose their lives (Acts 27:1–2, 21–24).

Judaism: Angels in the Old Testament are typically messengers of God. Two angels are mentioned by name in the Old Testament: Gabriel and Michael. Gabriel is a messenger and Michael is a warrior. Both are archangels. Angels were present at creation (Job 38:4, 7). An angel of the Lord found Hagar after Abraham cast her and Ishmael out (Genesis 16:7). Three angels visited Abraham on their way to Sodom (Genesis 18:2). Angels rescued Lot from the destruction of Sodom (Genesis 19:16). Angels stopped Abraham from sacrificing his son. Jacob wrestled with an angel (Genesis 32:22–32). Exodus 12 tells us of the Passover Angel. Deuteronomy 33:2 reveals angels were present when God gave the Law to Moses. An angel strengthened Elijah (1 Kings 19:5–7). The list of examples and angelic activity reveals that angels were active in the lives of Old Testament characters to direct, protect, and provide for.

Catholicism: Catholics believe angels are pure spirits God created, and they view angels in a similar way to Protestants: as attendants to God's throne, as God's messengers to mankind, and as personal guardians. Catholics also see angels as divine agents governing the world, and they believe in demon powers.[13]

Mormonism: According to the online Bible dictionary of the Church of Jesus Christ of Latter-Day Saints,[14] angels are messengers of the Lord. The dictionary says:

> We learn from latter-day revelation that there are two classes of heavenly beings who minister for the Lord: those who are spirits and those who have bodies of flesh and bone. Spirits are those beings who either have not yet obtained a body of flesh and bone (unembodied) or who have once had a mortal body and have died and are awaiting the Resurrection (disembodied). Ordinarily the word angel means those ministering persons who have a body of flesh and bone, being either resurrected from the dead (reembodied), or else translated, as were Enoch, Elijah, etc.

Islam: Islamic beliefs in angels are somewhat similar to those of Judaism and Christianity. Four angels stand out in Islam: Jibril (Gabriel), Mikal (Michael), Isra'il (the angel of death); and Israfil (the angel who puts souls in bodies and sounds the Last Judgment trumpet). Islam also believes demons contend for the souls of men, and they believe in a literal Satan, whom they call Iblis.[15]

Hinduism: Focused more on demons than angels, Hindus believe in *asuras*, demons that oppose their billion-plus gods. They specifically believe in serpent demons, a demon of drought, and an arch demon. Horrifying demons called *raksasas* linger in cemeteries, compel people to behave foolishly, and attack godly people, while *pisacas* demons haunt the scenes of violent deaths.[16]

Buddhism: Buddhists see demons as forces that keep them from reaching bliss, or Nirvana. They believe in an arch tempter called Mara and his daughters Rati, Raga, and Tanha, who work in unison against them. Like other Eastern religions, Buddhism focuses more on demons that prevent them from the "extinction of desire" than they do on angels.[17]

Nonliterate religions: Asia, Africa, Oceania, and the Americas generally classify the spirit world as good spirits or evil spirits, rather than angels and demons. Like ancient Greece and Rome, their beliefs align more with mythology, where certain gods can bring favor or calamity, than with anything that correlates to a biblical perspective.[18]

2

Angels: From History to Pop Culture

We don't know exactly when God created the angels, but we do know this: They were witnesses of creation. God created angels before He formed the foundations of the world with His words—and before He breathed made man in His own image.

We get some insight right from the Lord's own mouth in Job 38 verses 4 and 7 (NIV):

> *Where were you when I laid the earth's foundation?*
> *Tell me, if you understand...while the morning stars sang together*
> *and all the angels shouted for joy?*

Although they have not existed for all eternity like God Himself, angels may have existed for millions of years before the six days of creation listed in Genesis, considering that one of their primary roles in heaven is to worship around Father's throne. Angels cry:

Holy, holy, holy, is the Lord of Hosts;
the whole earth is full of His glory.

ISAIAH 6:3

When we consider that, with the Lord, one day is as a thousand years, and a thousand years as one day (2 Peter 3:8), determining when angels were created is an absolute mystery.

Angels first appear in Scripture in Genesis, when an angel of the Lord found Hagar by a spring of water in the wilderness after she fled from Sarah's harsh treatment (Genesis 16:7). The angel gave her a mighty promise from the Lord:

I will multiply your descendants exceedingly
so that they will be too many to count.

GENESIS 16:10

That promise was fulfilled through Ishmael.

All told, angels appear in Scripture more than two hundred times, and we'll study some of those encounters in the coming chapters. In this chapter, though, we'll look at why angels are so popular, the history of angels, angels and demons in pop culture, and widespread myths about the heavenly host in order to better understand how the perception of angels has evolved over the millennia, how the world sees angels, and how their assignment has been often misunderstood.

A BRIEF HISTORY OF CELESTIAL BEINGS

Before the image of angels as most Christians know them today came winged creatures of mythology. Nepthys, an ancient Egyptian spirit, had wings. Hermes was a messenger with wings on his heels in Greek mythology. Sumerians believed each person had a ghost as a constant companion, correlating to the more modern idea of guardian angels.

Then there's Zoroastrianism—a religion that predates both Christianity and Islam that is still alive in remote parts of Iran and India—founded by religious reformer Zarathustra. Zoroastrianism, which is thought to have influenced both Islam and Christianity, breaks down celestial beings into seven types of archangels that seem to inform New Age conceptions of angels: Archangel of Good Thought, Archangel of Right, Archangel of Dominion, Archangel of Piety, Archangel of Prosperity, Archangel of Immorality, and lower-ranking angels known as Lesser Ones.[19]

Across the annals of time, many faiths, cults, and societies have depicted winged creatures in the spirit realm. Of course, not all winged creatures are angels, and not all angels are winged creatures. That's fodder for another study. Indeed, throughout history, people have believed in ghosts, goblins, fairies, ghouls, and various evil spirits. As we just read, many of these beliefs are misinformed and misguided, as are modern beliefs about angels. Historically, angels have been largely misrepresented and misunderstood, even by those who read the Bible. Here's one truth to start with: Before the Holy Spirit inspired Scripture, angels existed. God created angels before He created the earth itself (Job 38:4, 7).

"The Bible tells us that the angels were created for one reason: to do God's will. To put it another way, they were created to be God's instruments or agents to carry out His work. (In fact, the word 'angel' actually means 'messenger' or 'agent'). The Bible says, 'Praise the Lord, you his angels, you mighty ones who do his bidding, who obey his word' (Psalm 103:20)," says evangelist Billy Graham.[20]

He continues:

> Just as the angels are largely unseen by us, so also is their work. I am convinced that when we get to heaven we will be amazed when we discover all the things God did through His angels—

including their protection over us in times of danger. (This includes not only physical danger, but moral and spiritual danger, as well.) The Bible says, "For he will command his angels concerning you to guard you in all your ways." (Psalm 91:11)[21]

WHY ARE ANGELS SO POPULAR?

Type "angels" into the search box on Amazon.com and you'll quickly find glass pocket guardian angels, angel figurines, angel tea lights, angel curio boxes, angel books, solar-powered angels with glowing dove LED lights, angel wind chimes, angel jewelry, angel throw blankets, light-up angel praying figures and—you get the idea.

Angels are popular in the retail world, the New Age world, the filmmaking world, and beyond. Baseball teams are named after them. Scholars debate them. Businesses incorporate angels in their branding. So-called angel investors fund businesses. The U.S. Navy has a Blue Angels division. And motorcycle enthusiasts have grouped together as Hells Angels.

The angel craze is very real. In fact, it's a little too real in Thailand, where a child angel phenomenon has people buying airplane tickets and reserving restaurant seats for dolls in a superstitious ritual that promises good luck. Thais carry child angels around as if they are living, breathing beings hoping for wealth, blessing, and protection.[22]

Mainline secular magazines and newspapers have penned stories and special reports on angels. *Time* magazine ran a cover story in December 1993 called "The New Age of Angels,"[23] later to follow up with an article titled "Guardian Angels Are Here, Say Most Americans."[24] *Redbook* magazine ran a story in January 2016 titled, "Is There an Angel Protecting the Baby in This Ultrasound?"[25] In 1994, ABC aired a two-hour, prime-time special called *Angels: The Mysterious Messengers*. The list goes on and on, even if the reporters and producers don't understand exactly what they are writing.

But why? Why are angels so popular—why have they been so popular throughout the ages with believers of many religions and unbelievers alike? What is it about angels, exactly, that so fascinates the world? Why do books about angels, demons, heaven, and hell continue to hit best-seller lists?

Ron Rhodes, president of Reasoning from the Scriptures Ministries and a regular on the Christian Research Institute's popular national radio broadcast, "The Bible Answer Man," offers some keen insights.[26] First, he points to the 1990s mega-best-selling fiction books, *This Present Darkness* and *Piercing the Darkness*. Frank Peretti's books offer graphic depictions of angelic intervention.

"Regardless of what one may think about the sensationalistic nature of these books, they certainly served to bring angels to the forefront in the minds of numerous Christians. Earlier, many had received a biblical crash course on this fascinating subject by reading Billy Graham's book, *Angels: God's Secret Agents*, which became one of the hottest-selling religious books of the 1970s," says Rhodes. He continues:

> New Agers have more recently become almost fanatically excited about angels because they have bought into a plethora of wildly unbiblical ideas about angels that nevertheless have great appeal in today's religious climate. One reason cited for angel popularity in New Age literature is that angels offer people a spirituality that does not involve commitment to God or His laws.
>
> Sophy Burnham, author of *A Book of Angels*, believes the current popularity of angels is "because we have created this concept of God as punitive, jealous, judgmental," while "angels never are. They are utterly compassionate." Or, as *Time* magazine put it, "For those who choke too easily on God and his rules...angels are the handy compromise, all fluff and meringue, kind, nonjudgmental. And they are available to everyone, like aspirin."

But there's a big problem with the angel craze. It's often riddled with error and smacks of the occult. John Ankerberg, founder and president of *The John Ankerberg Show* and coauthor of more than 158 books and study guides who holds three advanced degrees in theology, says what is most noteworthy about modern, popular idea of angels is their dissimilarity to the biblical presentation of angels:[27]

> The popular angels of today deny Christ's teachings, are related to the modern channeling movement and the world of the occult, seek to possess people, are very concerned about the environment in a pantheistic-nature worship sense, engage in distorting the Scriptures in their revelations, appear in near-death experiences, and perhaps not surprisingly, are very concerned with self-esteem/self-love teachings, the practice of divination and the "faith"/positive confession movement.
>
> In one sense, this is really nothing new; the spiritism that has been making its way into the American mainstream for the past 25 years has simply been repackaged in a more benevolent light. Put another way, the recent angel craze is simply occultism with a divine twist marketed under new management, so to speak.

ANGELS HAVE FASCINATED THE AGES

Interest in angels is more than a contemporary fad in the church and New Age world that inspires artists and impact our cultural landscape. A University of Michigan historian argues that angels stirred intense interest in the early years of Christianity as well.

"Just as many people today think of pets as part of their families, many people in the first 500 years of Christianity were convinced that angels were part of their lives,"[28] says Ellen Muehlberger, assistant professor of Near Eastern studies and history at the University of Michigan College of Literature, Science, and the Arts.

The Bible names various types of angels. Christians worked out what angels did and what they were during the fourth and fifth centuries, according to Muehlberger. She says an author living in Syria around the year 500 organized what little was known about angels into a "celestial hierarchy:" seraphim, cherubim, thrones, dominions, virtues, authorities, principalities, archangels, and angels.

In late antiquity, there was a much broader identity of angels than what we see in today's church. For example, Muehlberger notes, some believers referred to Christ as an angel or considered Christian ascetic monks who renounced family, food, drink, and sex and lived out in the desert were really angels. Of course, when the Egyptian monks learned they were being considered angels, they rejected the notion wholeheartedly.

Muehlberger recounts: "They said, 'We act like animals, not angels.'"[29] The monastic emphasis on humility was in direct conflict with the reputation ascetics had as special, holy people, equal to the angels, she explains, and exactly how angels looked and acted, and what humans could do to gain or lose their help was a frequent topic of debate. Most people did not envision angels looking the way we imagine them today—as beautiful winged creatures in diaphanous gowns.

"In antiquity, some Christians believed that angels were minds, or intellects, detached from bodies," Muehlberger says. "In a way, angels were like computers—very, very good at figuring things out and getting things done because they had rational minds but did not have the difficulty of having desires and passions, like humanity."[30]

One of the most widespread modern notions about angels emerged in the late-ancient era of Christianity that Muehlberger has studied. In those times, while some Christians assumed that guardian angels protected all human beings, others were convinced that angels were only given to those who had demonstrated their virtue. These were "companion angels," and not everyone had one.

"Certain monks in late ancient Egypt didn't believe that they were born with a guardian angel who watched over them throughout their lives. Instead, they expected to get a companion angel only as a reward for virtuous behavior," says Muehlberger. "Your companion angel was an assistant who could help you fight off demons, and only arrived if you proved yourself worthy. But if you went away from the community, into the village, and engaged in 'worldly' activities, that companion angel might leave you."[31]

EXPLORING ANGEL PERSONALITIES IN POP CULTURE

Exploring angels in pop culture offers some insight into why there are so many misconceptions about angels, even if it doesn't explain why the misconceptions exist. Angels have largely been stereotyped, and those stereotypes have evolved over the decades, it seems, to suit pop culture's fancy.

Let's start with films about angels, of which there have been more than forty. You may have seen some of the more popular ones. There's the classic Christmas favorite, *It's a Wonderful Life,* starring the late Jimmy Stewart as George Bailey, who stood at a bridge contemplating suicide. His guardian angel, Clarence Odbody, showed Bailey the many lives he touched. Old Clarence was innocent enough and probably did more to inspire faith that angels exist than propagate misperceptions about their interactions with humans. But not all films can claim this.

More recently, we saw angels appear in the $125 million biblical hit *Noah*, which stirred controversy by depicting fallen angels called Watchers. These Watchers are rock-monster creatures who come to earth to help men with special knowledge because they feel sorry they have to live "by the sweat of [their] brow." These Watchers are depicted with compassion that did not come from God's heart, leading them to disobey the Lord.

This concept seems to come from the Book of Enoch, which is not part of the canon of Scripture, yet Jude quotes from this book in verses 14–15. In any case, the Watcher angels in *Noah* defy Scripture and bring confusion about the work of angels in the time of the Flood and cast aspersions on angels by suggesting that fallen angels are good-natured, actually helped Noah build his famous ark, and died valiantly helping protect the ark from wicked human beings.

Likewise, television shows featuring angels abound, the most popular of which was *Touched by an Angel.* The show had a nine-year run on CBS, which offers this description of the supernatural drama series: "A beautiful, young earthbound angel named Monica and her down-to-earth supervisor Tess inspire people facing adversity to change their lives before it's too late. No matter how hopeless their circumstances, those who encounter Monica ultimately realize that they have been touched by an angel."[32] Though inspiring to many, *Touched by an Angel* fuels the false notion that there are female angels. There are no female angels or angels who manifest as females in Scripture.

Comic books and video games are facets of pop culture wherein angels appear over and again. Usually they are hybrid creatures with supernatural powers that look nothing like angels described in the Bible, but they do draw from some of their qualities. Role-playing board games like Dungeons & Dragons further propagate a New Age concept of angels with beings like Astral Deva, angels that watch over lesser beings from the heavens.

We can't leave out books in our exploration of angels in popular culture. A search on Amazon shows nearly twelve thousand "New Age & Spirituality" books about angels. There are more than 8,200 books in the "Angels & Spirit Guides" category. By contrast, there are only 568 "Christian Angeology & Demonology" books; 1,800 books on angels in the "Christian Living" category; 1,100 books in the "Christian Theology" category; and 334 in the "Bible Study category. It seems the world is more interested in angels than the church!

Beyond false religions, science fiction books have done perhaps the most to paint angels in an erroneous supernatural light. *Guardian Angel* by Anna Santos and Stefanie Shaw shows a protagonist who falls in love with her guardian angel, while Melissa Snark's *Prophecy: Novel of the Fallen Angels* is a profane, twisted portrayal of Nephilim descendants in modern times. And if that's not perverse enough, *Conspiracy of Angels* by Michelle Belanger features a character named Zach, who regains consciousness on Lake Erie to find a six-foot-six transsexual angel named Saliriel who explains angelic tribes trapped on earth. As you can see, popular culture is morphing angels to suit wicked agendas.

Finally, songs have done more than their part to shape our perception of angels. The late Jimi Hendrix, who died of a drug overdose, left behind a psychedelic rock anthem about an angel. Dubbed "Angel," the song speaks of a spirit being who descended from heaven to rescue someone. That's not altogether out of line with Scripture, as angels can deliver, but Hendrix depicts the angel as a woman. Madonna also performed a song called "Angel" in her debut album "Like a Virgin." The song speaks of an angelic encounter that lifts her spirits. The list of fictional angels in pop culture is long and has clearly shaped and molded our angelology.

A Revival of the Devil's Witchcraft in Media

Just as angels are painted with a humanistic brush in pop culture, demons are often glorified in mass media. Wikipedia actually publishes an A-to-Z list of fictional demons—there are nearly six hundred of them, and I imagine the list is not exhaustive. The online, crowd-sourced encyclopedia also offers a much shorter list of theological demons from various religions. Some demons made both lists.

Watching old videos of healing evangelists like Kathryn Kuhlman, A. A. Allen, Jack Coe, and Oral Roberts is one of my favorite things to do. I've consumed hundreds of hours of videos showing the miracle-working power of God and bold revival preaching that makes no apologies for the Rock of Offense. While watching an A. A. Allen miracle reel, my ears perked up when I heard the late Brother Allen declare a revival of the devil's witchcraft. Of course, this was back in the 1950s. What was a revival of witchcraft then has turned into a full-blown movement now.

"An awful lot of people are sick, diseased and afflicted under a curse, under a spell because of the present revival of witchcraft around the world," Allen declared. "There has never been a time in history when there has been such a devil's revival of witchcraft."

Think about it for a minute. In Allen's day, there was no such thing as *Harry Potter*. Allen made this declaration before popular TV shows like *Bewitched*, *Charmed*, and *The Witches of East End*—and before films like *Rosemary's Baby*, *The Blair Witch Project*, and *Season of the Witch*. Indeed, it was before children's media like *Meg and Mog*, *The Witch Family*, and *Witches in Stitches* hit the mainstream.

In recent years, we've seen the devil pressing hard to bring witchcraft deeper into our schools, our homes, and our entertainment venues. Through *Charisma News*, I've reported on how a new witchcraft-inspired challenge is luring kids into summoning demons. It's called Charlie Charlie, and it's sweeping the nation and the world under the guise of a carefree, fortune-telling game. Faith leaders are sounding the alarm.

I wrote about a new devil-inspired show called *Lucifer* on, of all stations, Fox. "Bored and unhappy as the lord of hell, Lucifer Morningstar has abandoned his throne and retired to L.A., where he owns Lux, an upscale nightclub," the show's description reads. "Charming, charismatic and devilishly handsome, Lucifer is enjoying his retirement, indulging in a few of his favorite things—wine, women and song—when a beautiful pop star is brutally murdered outside of Lux."[33]

Meanwhile, theaters in Miami put on a play based on John Van Druten's *Bell, Book and Candle*, which is about a witch who puts a love spell on a publisher who is soon to be engaged to his sweetheart. Of her new album, Florence and The Machine singer Florence Welch says she "got into obsessing about the LA witchcraft scene, and I was imagining this concept album about a witch trial in Hollywood, and someone falls in love."[34]

The devil is clearly driving toward a great awakening of the occult. This revival of the devil's witchcraft is unto an awakening to the occult that will set the very elect up to be deceived, it if is possible (see Matthew 24:24). False signs and wonders will rise, along with false prophets and false christs.

A generation of youth has been exposed to witchcraft games, television shows, movies, and more. The enemy is seducing people who are looking for the supernatural into a counterfeit movement that could have dangerous eternal outcomes. In the book of Revelation, God has made clear the fate of those who practice such things: Sorcerers will have their portion in the lake that burns with fire and brimstone (see Revelation 21:8). Let's keep pressing back this darkness.

How Demons Are Glorified in Mass Media

The devil is the prince of the power of the air, so it's not surprising that he would invade the entertainment and media mountains. At my count, there are well over one hundred films that glorify demons and the occult in some way, shape, or form. Blockbuster films like *Amityville Horror*, *Poltergeist*, *The Exorcist*, and *The Omen* terrified me as a child and fascinated the masses in the 1970s and 1980s. *The Exorcist* series has generated nearly half a billion dollars in revenues. There is a growing number of movies based on real-life cases of demonic possession, like *The Entity*, *The Serpent and the Rainbow*, and *The Possession.*

While the film world has banked on scary movies, the television world has been subtler in its workings to paint demons as friendly. Remember *Casper the Friendly Ghost*? *Buffy the Vampire Slayer* was popular in the 1990s, reaching four to six million viewers per episode. Buffy was guided by a watcher to slay vampires, demons, and other dark forces. The concept spun off into novels, comic books, and video games.

Of course, *The X-Files*, which explored strange and unexplained cases while hidden forces worked to hinder their efforts, was one of the most popular TV shows of the 1990s. Also in the 1990s, *Charmed* featured three sisters who discovered their destiny—to battle against forces of evil with witchcraft. Sort of ironic, I know.

Long before all this, shows like *The Twilight Zone* spooked audiences. I already mentioned *Bewitched.* The 1960s also saw the rise of shows like *The Munsters,* with grandpa practicing witchcraft; *The Addams Family,* with the slim witch Morticia concocting potions; and *I Dream of Jeannie*—all of which were also skews on reality that opened the door to the dark side of the supernatural through humor.

"Undoubtedly, dark-themed entertainment, in the form of movies, books, television shows, and video games, is here to stay," said Samuel C. Baxter, writing for *The Real Truth* magazine.[35] "Publishing houses and film studios have turned this pop-culture phenomenon into a multibillion-dollar industry. Take vampires, for example. *DailyFinance* estimates that movies, television series, books, magazines and costumes for fanged 'creatures of the night' constitute at least a $10 billion industry in the United States. For audiences worldwide, this sort of entertainment has an unmistakable draw."[36]

Demons often take center stage in comic books, from *Hellboy* and *Ghost Rider* to *Spawn* and *Ertigan* and beyond. These superheroes from hell have muddied what was once a world dominated by the likes of good guys like Superman, Batman, and Spiderman. This has spilled over into videogames that feature demons in starring roles, including The Devil Inside, Devil May Cry, Demon Gaze, Demon's Crest, Demon's Souls, and Daemonica. But board games are also propagating a fascination with demons. I mentioned Dungeon & Dragons, but classic Ouija boards have been around for decades. Consider this report from the Barna Group:

> Teenagers relish experiences and the supernatural world provides fertile ground for their explorations. In fact, three-quarters of America's youth (73%) have engaged in at least one type of psychic or witchcraft-related activity, beyond mere media exposure or horoscope usage.
>
> The most common types of witchcraft behaviors were using a Ouija board and reading a book about witchcraft or Wicca, each of which had been done by more than one-third of teenagers. More than one-quarter of teens have played a game featuring sorcery or witchcraft elements. One-tenth of teens had participated in a séance and 1 out of 12 had tried to cast a spell or mix a magic potion.
>
> As for psychic activities, more than one-fourth of teens have had their palm read (30%) or their fortune told (27%). Other psychic deeds included being physically present when someone else used psychic powers (14%), visiting a medium or spiritual guide (9%), and consulting a psychic (9%).
>
> Walking the line between entertainment and spiritual experimentation, 4 out of every 5 teens have read their horoscope before—and say they do so "just for fun." The new resource points out that while most teens are not convinced that horoscopes are always accurate, more than one-quarter believes they are always or usually true. Only a minority of teens believes that horoscopes are not at all accurate and should be avoided.[37]

Books starring demons and the occult are massively popular. The best-selling nonfiction book *Beware the Night* was adapted into a movie called *Deliver Us from Evil.* Airport bookstores report strong sales of Dan Brown's *Angels & Demons,* a prequel to the #1 New York Times best-seller, *The Da Vinci Code.* With perversion rising, we're even seeing recommended paranormal romance novels. According to Amazon, *Name Your Demon* is "an urban fantasy and paranormal romance collection showcasing 15 first-in-series reads from *New York Times, USA Today,* and International Bestselling Authors."[38]

Dark literature, of course, is nothing new. The Brothers Grimm offered some especially dark folk tales in the 1800s. Snow White was the victim of child abuse. Cinderella's story was marked by graphic violence. Hansel and Gretel's evil stepmother planned to boil the young boy alive. Then there's Edgar Allen Poe, with his dark poems like "Spirits of the Dead" and "The Raven."

WHEN THE MUSIC INDUSTRY GLORIFIES DEMONS

Secular music is filled with demon glorification. And it didn't just start with playing songs from Led Zeppelin that revealed hidden messages that appear to say, "Oh here's to my sweet Satan. The one whose little path would make me sad, whose power is Satan. He will give those with him 666. There was a little tool shed where he made us suffer, sad Satan" (from "Stairway to Heaven."[39])

Whether or not that was Zeppelin founder, songwriter, and guitarist Jimmy Page's intent—he's denied it—the classic rock legend owned an occult bookstore in the '70s, and both classic and modern rock have plenty of occult elements.

Although I don't believe all secular music is inherently evil—some secular music has a more positive message than Christian songs I hear, and not all "Christian" songs are birthed by the Spirit of God or performed by actual Christians—I don't listen to secular radio. I haven't listened to secular radio on purpose since I was saved and tossed thousands of dollars worth of secular CDs in the garbage.

As dark as secular music was when I was growing up in the Goth and Grunge age, mainstream music has taken on a whole new level of demonic influence as popular radio songs work to get our youth to confess they are demon inspired, if not demon possessed.

This revelation came as I was driving across the state of Florida with my teenage daughter and decided to listen to what type of music today's youth finds appealing. I heard the typical Miley Cyrus and Katy Perry hits that were hardly wholesome but not especially wicked. But I also heard tunes from "artists" like Eminem, Rihanna, and Imagine Dragons that shocked me.

Consider the hook in Eminem's "The Monster," which features Rihanna: "I'm friends with the monster that's under my bed; Get along with the voices inside of my head; You're trying to save me, stop holding your breath; And you think I'm crazy, yeah, you think I'm crazy."[40]

Then there's Imagine Dragons, with its "Demons" hit that talks about the "beast inside" and proclaims, "No matter what we breed; We still are made of greed; This is my kingdom come; This is my kingdom come" and then goes on to declare, "When you feel my heat; Look into my eyes; It's where my demons hide; It's where my demons hide; Don't get too close; It's dark inside; It's where my demons hide; It's where my demons hide."[41]

And this is what much of today's youth is listening to—rock stars confessing and glorifying their struggles with voices in their heads and demons in their souls. Even church kids are listening to this demon-inspired drivel, singing right along with Rihanna and Imagine Dragons, agreeing they have voices in their heads and demons in their souls when they should be agreeing with the voice of God and the Holy Spirit about who He is.

You might say to me, "Jennifer, this is nothing new."

Maybe not.

But the beats and lyrics of modern secular music are growing darker. We've moved from "Amazing Grace," with its "how sweet the sound" lyric to Electric Hellfire Club with songs like "Kiss the Goat." I know there's plenty of satanic underground heavy metal music that never makes it onto the radio, but clearly, Satan, who once led worship in heaven, or his demons are dropping lyrics into the minds of pop stars who have a mainstream radio platform. The key word is "mainstream." This isn't some dark underground music I'm talking about. These are top hits.

What's the danger?

According to an Illinois State University study, male undergraduates behaved with more hostility toward women and were more likely to view aggressive behavior positively after viewing music videos that featured violent acts. And an Emory University Study reveals black girls between the ages of 14 and 18 who viewed hardcore rap videos for fourteen hours a week or more were three times more likely to hit a teacher, two and one-half times more likely to get arrested, and one and one-half times more likely to get a sexually transmitted disease, use drugs, or drink alcohol.

Of course, there's no particular study about what happens to teens who confess there are voices inside their head and demons hiding inside them. But a spiritually minded person can connect the dots, and the final picture is disturbing. The power of death and life are in the tongue (Proverbs 18:21). A generation of youth is confessing insanity and demon possession over their lives.

Again, you're probably saying, "This is nothing new." Maybe not. And maybe there's nothing we can do to stop today's youth from confessing they have voices inside of their head and demons inside while they are riding in the car with their friends or even sitting in their rooms with an iPod and headphones blaring the demonic messages in their ears.

But that doesn't mean we shouldn't be vigilant. That doesn't mean we shouldn't teach our youth the spiritual implications of singing along with their favorite heathen rappers. That doesn't mean we should allow the music in our homes and cars. That doesn't mean we should bury our heads in the sand while a generation of youth is confessing demon possession and insanity, does it?

During a performance of her song "Haunted," Beyoncé's hair got caught up on her earring, tearing it from her ear and causing plenty of blood—and a call to cut. After the performance, Twitter and Facebook were ablaze with "#CutforBeyonce" and "BleedforBeyonce" hashtags. The so-called Beyhive—a name that describes the once-Christian singer's fan base of mostly women and gay men who obsess over her stardom—started cutting themselves in a show of unity with the singer.

This is not speculation. Gruesome, bloody photos have cropped up on social media revealing that Beyoncé's fans are bleeding for her, along with comments like these:

"If the queen bleeds the hive must unify and leak our blood to restore her spirits," one super fan tweeted. "Beyhive we must."[42]

"If Queen B had to endure pain, so do I. Tonight we #Cutfor Beyonce."[43]

Cutting is a dark trend that's suddenly making its way into the limelight. Indeed, the #CutforBieber and #Cut4Bieber hashtags have been trending on Twitter, a social media platform of choice for teens.

Let's step back for a minute. What is cutting? And how serious is it? Cutting is a form of deliberate self-harm, self-inflicted violence in which people take a razor blade or other sharp object and cut into their flesh to the point of letting blood.

The psychology behind it is heart-wrenching: The pain of cutting is a distraction from the emotional pain, anger, and frustration the cutter feels. The cutters may slice their wrists, arms, legs, or stomachs. The cuts are often so deep they leave scars that mirror the emotional scars in their soul.

I've been involved with youth who call themselves cutters. So when

I saw this campaign of the "Beyhive," it struck my heart. Encouraging anyone to cut, even in a mock protest, is more than irresponsible. It's a demon-inspired ploy to drive depressed teenagers deeper into bondage and lure curious youth to engage in an act they've never had the courage to act out.

Cutting is indeed a serious problem, but because cutters tend to hide their self-injury, it often goes unnoticed and is difficult to track. *The Journal of Clinical Psychology* reports about 4 percent of the U.S. population show signs of self-injurious behavior. That's more than twelve million people. A cnn.com poll shows that one in five teens has purposely injured his or her own self at some time.

Although self-injury may bring a momentary sense of calm and a release of tension, the Mayo Clinic reports it's usually followed by guilt, shame, and the return of painful emotions. And, Mayo reports, with self-injury comes the possibility of more serious and even fatal self-aggressive actions. Make no mistake: Even though the cutter's intent is not suicide, cutters could take the practice down the dark road to death, even accidentally.

If you think your teen—or someone you know—is cutting, consider the signs and symptoms the Mayo Clinic lists, which include scars, fresh cuts, scratches, bruises, and other wounds; possession of sharp objects; wearing long sleeves or long pants (even in hot weather); spending a lot of time alone; claiming to have frequent accidents; behavioral or emotional instability; and statements of helplessness or hopelessness.

Teens are good at hiding what's going on in their hearts. If you think someone is cutting, seek out help from a pastor, school counselor, or pediatrician. To Write Love on Her Arms offers valuable insights. Cutting is no laughing matter, and I pray that all young ones who are caught up in cutting will find healing for their wounded hearts. And Twitter, if you are listening, I urge you to find a way to cut off these types of campaigns before copycat mockers find a new platform from which to spread their potentially deadly messages.

What the Bible Says About Celebrating Darkness

The Bible clearly speaks against engaging in darkness, much less celebrating it. Yet Western culture is riddled with mediums and necromancers, sorcerers, fortune-tellers, and omens. All of this is rooted in manifestations of the demonic. Let's look at just a few Scriptures to support the absolute shunning of anything that smells like the demonic:

Leviticus 19:31 reads, "Do not turn to spirits through mediums or necromancers. Do not seek after them to be defiled by them: I am the Lord your God." A medium is someone who communicates with demon spirits, often called familiar spirits. The witch at Endor tapped into familiar spirits when she conjured up what looked like Samuel at King Saul's command (1 Samuel 28:7). Necromancy, on the other hand, as defined by *Merriam-Webster*, is a "conjuration of the spirits of the dead for purposes of magically revealing the future or influencing the source of events."

Leviticus 20:6 says, "The person who turns to spirits through mediums and necromancers in order to whore after them, I will even set My face against that person and will cut him off from among his people." Can you imagine whoring after a demon? Paul told the church at Ephesus, "And do not have fellowship with the unfruitful works of darkness; instead, expose them. For it is shameful even to speak of those things which are done by them in secret. But all things are exposed when they are revealed by the light, for everything that becomes visible is light. Therefore He says: 'Awake, you who sleep, arise from the dead, and Christ will give you light'" (Ephesians 5:11–14).

Exodus 22:18 says, "You must not allow a sorceress to live." Again, we're in an age of grace and Jesus came to save the world, not condemn it (John 3:16). But the reality is those who don't repent of these wicked practices will not meet a welcome fate. Revelation 21:8 tells us plainly, "But the cowardly, the unbelieving, the abominable, the murderers, the sexually immoral, the sorcerers, the idolaters, and all liars shall have their portion in the lake which burns with fire and brimstone. This is the second death."

Scripture reveals repeatedly how the Lord feels about engaging with demons in whatever manifestation. Satan has worked to deceive the lost and even many who have accepted Christ as Lord and Savior into celebrating demons through media. What we need is a transforming revival like we saw in Ephesus. We find the account in Acts 19:11–20:

> God worked powerful miracles by the hands of Paul. So handkerchiefs or aprons he had touched were brought to the sick, and the diseases left them, and the evil spirits went out of them.
>
> Then some of the itinerant Jewish exorcists invoked the name of the Lord Jesus over those who had evil spirits, saying, "We command you to come out in the name of Jesus whom Paul preaches." There were seven sons of a Jewish high priest named Sceva doing this. The evil spirit answered, "I know Jesus, and I know Paul, but who are you?" Then the man in whom the evil spirit was jumped on them, overpowered them, and prevailed against them, so that they fled from that house naked and wounded.
>
> This became known to all Jews and Greeks living in Ephesus. And fear fell on them all, and the name of the Lord Jesus was magnified. Many who believed came confessing and telling their deeds. Many who practiced magic brought their books together and burned them before everyone. They calculated their value, which equaled fifty thousand drachmas. So the word of the Lord powerfully grew and spread.

When the power of God manifests—and when angels manifest—it gets the attention of the lost and saved alike. As we pray for the next great move of God and the great harvest that will come along with it, we also need to press into signs, wonders, and miracles that defy the power of the enemy. In 1 Corinthians 14:1, inspired by the Holy Spirit, Paul admonishes us to:

> *Follow after love and desire spiritual gifts,*
> *but especially that you may prophesy.*

The word for "desire" in the Greek is *zeloo*. According to the *KJV New Testament Greek Lexicon*, it's a pretty intense feeling. It means: "to burn with zeal; in a good sense, to be zealous in the pursuit of good; desire earnestly; pursue." *Merriam-Webster* defines "zeal" as "a strong feeling of interest and enthusiasm that makes someone very eager or determined to do something." Let's get determined to understand how to cooperate with the Spirit of God—and His angels—to see a Third Great Awakening.

3

Fact and Fiction about Angels

Many Christians around the world misunderstand what angels do—and what they don't do. Many have misperceptions, misunderstandings, misapprehensions, and even delusions about angels. The pop culture portrayal—and false religion's portrayal—of angels has opened the door to plenty of myths about these heavenly creatures.

You may even believe some of these myths yourself. The truth is you don't know what you don't know. False teachings about angels can hinder you from embracing the work of angels on assignment. In this chapter, we'll explore the most common myths about angels and drill into some Bible truths about angels you need to keep in mind as you discern angels on assignment.

Myth #1: Angels are essentially good. God is good and He created every angel that exists, but not all angels are good. Once the worship leader in heaven, Lucifer went astray with pride. In Luke 10:18, Jesus told His disciples, "I saw Satan as lightning fall from heaven." Jesus was referring to something Isaiah described in his book:

How are you fallen from heaven, O Lucifer, son of the morning! How you are cut down to the ground, you who weaken the nations! For you have said in your heart, "I will ascend into heaven, I will exalt my throne above the stars of God; I will sit also on the mount of the congregation, in the recesses of the north; I will ascend above the heights of the clouds, I will be like the Most High." Yet you shall be brought down to Hell, to the sides of the pit.

ISAIAH 14:12–15

Revelation 12:4 also points to this day, when a third of the angels joined Lucifer (Satan) in his insurrection against the Creator of the Universe:

His tail drew a third of the stars of heaven,
and threw them to the earth.

Satan is the Father of lies (John 8:44). Peter calls him our adversary and warns that the devil is roaming about like a roaring lion seeking someone to devour (1 Peter 5:8). Satan disguises himself as an angel of light (2 Corinthians 11:14). Jesus called him a thief who comes to steal, kill, and destroy (John 10:10). Paul speaks of standing against the schemes of the devil (Ephesians 6:11). Satan, the god of this world, blinds the minds of unbelievers (2 Corinthians 4:4). Indeed, the world lies in the power of the evil one (1 John 5:19).

And remember, it's not just Satan who is an evil angel. One-third of the angels in heaven followed him. Paul warns:

For we are not wrestling with flesh and blood [contending only with physical opponents], but against the despotisms, against the powers, against [the master spirits who are] the world rulers of this present darkness, against the spirit forces of wickedness in the heavenly (supernatural) sphere.

EPHESIANS 6:12, AMPC

Myth #2: There are baby angels. Historic and modern art like to show angels like babies or little children with wings. They look sweet and innocent, but cherubs are not baby angels. Cherubim in the Bible are winged angels that attend to God. Cherubim worship and praise God. We read in Genesis 3:24:

> *So he drove out the man; and he placed at the east of the garden of Eden Cherubims, and a flaming sword which turned every way, to keep the way of the tree of life.*

Do we really think God is going to use baby angels with cute smiles as sentinels? Before his fall, Satan was a cherubim angel. He's not a baby boy turned evil.

Myth #3: Angels can be male or female. This myth seems to have originated from historical paintings of winged creatures that appeared as women and little girls. Angels appear as males with male clothing and male names in Scripture (Genesis 18:2, Ezekiel 9:2). The only named angels in the Bible are Michael, Gabriel, and, of course, Lucifer.

Nowhere in the Old Testament do we see angels in the context of being female or even gender neutral. The Greek word for "angel"—*angelos*—in the New Testament takes on the masculine form, and there is no corresponding feminine form of the word. There is not one single scriptural reference to a female angel.

The Zechariah 5:9 argument for female angels is flawed. Let's look at that Scripture:

> *Then I lifted my eyes and saw coming forward two women. There was wind in their wings, and the wings were like those of a stork, and they lifted up and carried the ephah basket between heaven and earth.*

The problem with the argument is Zechariah does not identify these beings as angels, but as winged creatures.

Myth #4: Angels should be worshipped. Angels should not be worshipped and indeed they do not want our worship. Paul explained to the church at Colossae:

> *Do not let anyone cheat you of your reward by delighting in false humility and the worship of angels, dwelling on those things which he has not seen, vainly arrogant due to his unspiritual mind, and not supporting the head, from which the entire body, nourished and knit together by joints and sinews, grows as God gives the increase.*
>
> COLOSSIANS 2:18–19

We also see John twice bowing down before angels in the book of Revelation, and the angels shunning his adoration. Let's look at both encounters:

> *I fell at [the angel's] feet to worship him. But he said to me, "See that you not do that. I am your fellow servant, and of your brothers who hold the testimony of Jesus. Worship God! For the testimony of Jesus is the spirit of prophecy."*
>
> REVELATION 19:10

> *I, John, am he who saw and heard these things. When I heard and saw them, I fell down to worship at the feet of the angel who showed me these things. But he said to me, "See that you not do that. For I am your fellow servant, and of your brothers the prophets, and of those who keep the words of this book. Worship God!"*
>
> REVELATION 22:9

Myth #5: There is an angel of death. The Grim Reaper is popular in our culture, representing the angel of death carrying a sickle and wearing a dark cloak. But we can't find an angel of death in the Bible. Many have had encounters of angels escorting them to heaven in the afterlife, but this is not the angel of death pop culture likes to propagate.

Myth #6: Angels only save lives, but don't take them. Although there is not an angel of death in the Bible, we do see the Lord sends angels on assignment to bring death. Here is one striking account during a battle between the Israalites and the Assyrians:

> *On that night the angel of the Lord went out and struck one hundred and eighty-five thousand in the camp of the Assyrians. When others woke up early in the morning, these were all dead bodies. So Sennacherib king of Assyria departed and stayed in Nineveh.*
>
> 2 KINGS 19:35–36

Myth #7: Angels have halos. Artists tend to paint angels—and even Jesus—with a halo. But you can't find halos in the Bible. Halos are a cultural idea that we see in the art of Egyptians and Romans. What is depicted in those images is actually called a nimbus, which *Merriam-Webster* defines as "a luminous vapor, cloud, or atmosphere about a god or goddess when on earth: a cloud or atmosphere (as of romance) about a person or thing; an indication (as a circle) of radiant light or glory about the head of a drawn or sculptured divinity, saint, or sovereign." This was not a biblical idea. It's an expression in the art world.

Myth #8: All angels have two wings. The art world loves to paint angels with wings—usually a human figure with two wings. But this is not purely biblical. Although angels do appear as humans, nowhere in the Word of God do human figures appear with wings—and only two types of angelic beings in the Bible have wings. How many wings do they have? Seraphim have six wings (Isaiah 6:1–3). Cherubim have four (Ezekiel 1:11).

Myth #9: Angels were humans first. Angels may take on human form when they manifest in the earth, but make no mistake—angels are not humans and were never humans and will never be humans. When we die, we don't become angels. Psalm 8:5 says:

For You have made him a little lower than the angels,
and crowned him with glory and honor.

And Hebrews 2:7 quotes the psalmist.

Myth #10: Angels are merely a New Age trend. Hopefully by now, you understand this is a myth. The New Age movement is one of the top disinformation sources of angels in the world. The New Age movement talks about angels, as well as personal guides, teachers, contacts, and masters—all spirit beings. New Agers also speak of channeling, astrological cycles, the Age of Aquarius, and other terms that are unbiblical. New Agers name angels all sorts of strange names that violate Scripture. The bottom line is that God created angels before New Age thinking ever existed.

Myth #11: Angels will stop you from sinning. God created us with a free will. He allows us to choose whether or not we obey His commands (Deuteronomy 30:19–20). If God Himself is not going to stop us from sinning, His angels certainly will not.

These are some of the top myths concerning angels. There are many others that are probably too obscure for most reasonable people to believe. But what about the truths?

Truth #1: Angels obey the Lord's commands, not ours. I hear many, especially spiritual warriors, "commanding" angels. I cannot find anywhere in Scripture that says we are to "command" angels. Psalm 91:11 (AMP) says:

For He will command His angels in regard to you, To protect and defend and guard you in all your ways [of obedience and service].

And Psalm 103:20 states:

Bless the Lord, you His angels, who are mighty,
and do His commands, and obey the voice of His word.

Truth #2: Angels have a free will. Like humans, angels are not robots. We know that one-third of the angels followed Lucifer (Satan) in his insurrection and were cast of heaven with him. Jude 6 tells us plainly:

Likewise, the angels who did not keep to their first domain, but forsook their own dwelling, He has kept in everlasting chains under darkness for the judgment of the great day.

Angels choose to serve the living God, just as we do.

Truth #3: We have angels. In Matthew 18:10, Jesus said:

See that you do not despise one of these little ones.
For I say to you that in Heaven their angels always see
the face of My Father who is in Heaven.

We see angelic activity in the New Testament was common. When Peter was released from prison (by an angel) he came knocking on the door where intercessors were praying for his release—but they didn't believe when he actually showed up. They said it was his angel (see Acts 12:15). The Bible says angels are ministering spirits to those who inherit salvation (Hebrews 1:14).

Truth #4: Angels never die. Luke 20:36 says:

For they cannot die any more, for they are equal to the angels
and are the sons of God, being sons of the resurrection.

Truth #5: Angels serve as deliverers. Although God is our fortress, our strength and our deliverer, He can choose to send angels with deliverance assignments. Psalm 34:7 bears this out:

The angel of the Lord camps around those
who fear Him, and delivers them.

Truth #6: Angels can speak with a loud voice. Revelation 7:2 reveals:

And I saw another angel ascending from the east, having the seal of the living God. He cried out with a loud voice to the four angels who had been given power to harm the earth and the sea.

Truth #7: Angels have strong discernment. Second Samuel 14:17 says:

So, your servant thought, "May the word of my lord the king provide rest. For like the angel of God, my lord the king discerns good from evil. May the Lord your God be with you."

Truth #8: Angels worship God. The angels in heaven worship God. We see this several times in Scripture. Isaiah the prophet offers a stunning visual that took place as part of his commissioning:

In the year that King Uzziah died I saw the Lord sitting on a throne, high and lifted up, and His train filled the temple. Above it stood the seraphim. Each one had six wings. With two he covered his face, and with two he covered his feet, and with two he flew. One cried to another and said: "Holy, holy, holy, is the Lord of Hosts; the whole earth is full of His glory."

ISAIAH 6:1–3

Consider this spectacular scene of over one hundred million angels worshipping the Lord, as John describes in Revelation 5:11–13:

Then I looked, and I heard around the throne and the living creatures and the elders the voices of many angels, numbering ten thousand times ten thousand, and thousands of thousands, saying with a loud voice: "Worthy is the Lamb who was slain, to receive power and riches and wisdom and strength and honor and glory and blessing!" Then I heard every creature which is in heaven and on the earth and under the earth and in the sea, and all that are in them, saying: "To Him who sits on the throne and to the Lamb be blessing and honor and glory and power, forever and ever!"

We see a similar scene in Revelation 4:8:

All day and night, without ceasing, they were saying:
"Holy, holy, holy, Lord God Almighty,"
who was, and is, and is to come.

Then again in Revelation 7:11–12:

All the angels stood around the throne and the elders and the four living creatures and fell on their faces before the throne and worshipped God, "Amen! Blessing and glory and wisdom and thanksgiving and honor and power and might be to our God forever and ever! Amen."

Angels worship God and God alone. There is no idolatry in the heavenly angelic host. They never grow weary of worship. They are not distracted in worship by the turkey in the oven at home. Even though they can't quite comprehend the work of the cross or the redemption in the blood of Christ, they find plenty of reasons to worship God. First and foremost, I believe, is that they better understand His wisdom, His beauty, His character, and His holiness.

Truth #9: Angels will declare the end times. Angels play a pivotal role in the end times by making various announcements. We see one example in Revelation 10:5–7:

The angel whom I saw standing on the sea and on the earth lifted up his hand to heaven and swore by Him who lives forever and ever, who created heaven and the things that are in them, and the earth and the things that are in it, and the sea and the things that are in it, that there should be no more delay. But in the days when the seventh angel is about to sound, the mystery of God will be fulfilled, as He has declared to His servants the prophets.

Matthew Henry's Commentary explains the significance of these end-times messenger angels:

> The matter of the oath: that there shall be time no longer; either, (1.) That there shall be now no longer delay in fulfilling the predictions of this book than till the last angel should sound; then every thing should be put into speedy execution: the mystery of God shall be finished, Rev. 10:7. Or, (2.) That when this mystery of God is finished time itself shall be no more, as being the measure of things that are in a mutable changing state; but all things shall be at length for ever fixed, and so time itself swallowed up in eternity.

Truth #10: Angels can see the face of God. John the apostle tells us:

No one has seen God at any time. The only Son, who is at the Father's side, has made Him known.

JOHN 1:18

Although the Bible says Moses spoke to God face to face, this was a figure of speech to portray the intimacy the prophet had with His creator.

When Moses asked the Lord to show him His glory, God's response was telling:

"I will make all My goodness pass before you, and I will proclaim the name of the Lord before you. I will be gracious to whom I will be gracious and will show mercy on whom I will show mercy." He said, "You cannot see My face, for no man can see Me and live." Then the Lord said, "Indeed, there is a place by Me. You must stand on the rock. While My glory passes by, I will put you in a cleft of the rock and will cover you with My hand while I pass by. Then I will take away My hand, and you will see My back, but My face may not be seen."

EXODUS 33:19–23

People may have dreams and visions of Jesus. God appears as the angel of the Lord (Judges 13:22), but we don't see God face to face. The angels see the face of God:

See that you do not despise one of these little ones.
For I say to you that in heaven their angels
always see the face of My Father who is in heaven.

MATTHEW 18:10

One day, though, we will see our Bridegroom, King, and Judge face to face.

Paul writes:

For now we see as through a glass, dimly, but then, face to face.
Now I know in part, but then I shall know, even as I also am known.

1 CORINTHIANS 13:12

And John writes:

Beloved, now are we children of God, and it has not yet been revealed what we shall be. But we know that when He appears, we shall be like Him, for we shall see Him as He is.

1 JOHN 3:2

I imagine in that day, we'll join with the worshipping angels crying, "holy, holy, holy."

Truth #11: Angels gather our prayers. Revelation 8:3 tells us:

Another angel, having a golden censer, came and stood at the altar.
He was given much incense to offer with the prayers of
all the saints on the golden altar which was before the throne.

This is one way ministering spirits serve us.

Truth #12: Angels rejoice when someone gets saved. Luke 15:10 reveals:

There is joy in the presence of the angels
of God over one sinner who repents.

Why are the angels rejoicing? Because the devil lost and Jesus wins. They are celebrating the victory of the risen Lamb, who offers salvation unto men who will eternally worship the King of glory.

Truth #13: Angels can appear as people. Angels are invisible until God chooses to have them reveal themselves to humans. Often, in these instances the angels appear in human form. Hebrews 13:2 warns:

Do not forget to entertain strangers,
for thereby some have entertained angels unknowingly.

Truth #14: Angels can be assigned to nations. Daniel 12:1 tells us:

And at that time Michael shall stand up,
the great prince who stands guard over the sons of your people.

Angels can be assigned to guard nations. At the same time, fallen angels—or principalities—can be assigned over nations as well.

In the nook of Daniel, we are told of a battle between Michael and an evil angel working to thwart the delivery of his prayer answers:

> *Then he said to me, "Do not be afraid, Daniel. For from the first day that you set your heart to understand this and to humble yourself before your God, your words were heard, and I have come because of your words. But the prince of the kingdom of Persia withstood me for twenty-one days. So Michael, one of the chief princes, came to help me, for I had been left there with the kings of Persia."*
>
> DANIEL 10:12–13

Truth #15: Angels are holy. Matthew 25:31 says:

> *When the Son of Man comes in His glory,*
> *and all the holy angels with Him,*
> *then He will sit on the throne of His glory.*

We know God is holy. We know Jesus was sinless—holy—when He walked the earth. We know, of course, that the Holy Spirit is holy. But we should also keep in mind that God's angels are holy. The Greek word used to describe the holiness of angels in this verse is *haigos*. It means "set apart by (or for) God, holy, sacred." HELPS Word-studies explains that it means "properly, different (unlike), other ('otherness')."

4

People Are Seeing Angels Everywhere

Angels are everywhere—and people are reporting angel sightings with more frequency than I've ever witnessed. Believers and unbelievers alike are pointing to the manifestation of angels in various forms. Some are even hearing angels singing. Surprisingly, secular news media outlets are documenting the reports.

That said, angel sightings are nothing new. The Bible records plenty of angel sightings that set a precedent for what we are seeing and reading about today. Before we turn to some modern-day chronicles of angel sightings, it's important to establish this pattern in the Bible to build our faith for what seems to be unlikely or impossible to some. These aren't merely angels in a vision or a dream—which are also found in Scripture—but accounts of people in Scripture who actually saw angels with their own two eyes.

Hagar saw an angel by a spring of water in the wilderness (Genesis 16:7). Lot saw two angels while he was sitting at the gate of Sodom (Genesis 19:1). Moses saw an angel in the form of a flaming fire in the midst of a bush (Exodus 3:2). A donkey saw an angel of the Lord with a sword drawn in His hand (Numbers 22:23), then Balaam, who was riding the donkey also saw him (Numbers 22:31). Gideon saw an angel of the Lord, who called him a mighty man of valor (Judges 6:12).

Although many of these sightings turned into encounters, not all angel sightings are encounters. Elisha once asked the Lord to open His servant's eyes so he could see into the spirit realm, and he saw the mountain was full of horses and chariots of fire surrounding them (2 Kings 6:17). His servant saw the Lord's angel armies. When Jacob was preparing to meet his estranged brother Esau, whose birthright he stole, Jacob saw the angels of God (Genesis 32:1).

Angels can manifest in many ways. Many times in Scripture, angels look like men. (Genesis 18:2; Judges 13:6; Mark 16:5, and Luke 24:4 are just a few examples.) Angels have also appeared in brilliance or light (see Matthew 28:3, Acts 1:10, Ezekiel 1:13, Daniel 10:6, and John 20:12). Psalm 104:4 reveals that God:

> *...makes His angels as winds, His ministers as a flaming fire.*

Other than in dreams and visions, it's important to note that angels in Scripture do not appear as winged creatures or as female. Female winged creations in Zechariah 5:9 were not called angels, but winged creatures.

WHEN ANGELS ARE CAUGHT ON CAMERA

Some claim to have caught angel sightings on camera, like Erin Potter. The Kirtland, Ohio, girl was battling leukemia. A photo of Erin running with sparklers in her hands in the backyard reveals what appears to be an angel standing right behind her. The young girl had a bone marrow transplant shortly after the incident and today is cancer-free.

"I know she's not alone, I know we are not alone and people who don't want to believe it, that's OK," Kevin Potter told KPTV. "Whatever happened, you know something powerful and special was there with us."[44]

The Today Show reported the story of a 14-year-old girl hospitalized, dying with pneumonia. Just as her mother expected her to breathe her last breath, she saw a bright white light on a security monitor. The dying girl started to recover within an hour, with no medical explanation. Her mother, Colleen, convinced that "this was an image of an angel," called the healing "a miracle."[45]

The Bible does speak of angels involved in healing in John 5. John the apostle writes about a pool called Bethesda near the Sheep Gate in Jerusalem. Sick people gathered there—some blind, some crippled, and some paralyzed—waiting for the troubling of the water. John 5:4 says, "For an angel went down at a certain time into the pool and stirred up the water. After the stirring of the water, whoever stepped in first was healed of whatever disease he had."

The Bible also speaks of a great cloud of witnesses, just after the recount of names in the Hall of Faith. Hebrews 12 declares:

> *Therefore, since we are encompassed with such a great cloud of witnesses, let us also lay aside every weight and the sin that so easily entangles us, and let us run with endurance the race that is set before us.*

This great cloud of witnesses directly speaks of saints who have walked before us, yet we know that the angel watchers are also observing.

But do angels appear in clouds? Many believe they do. They point to Revelation 10:1, which reads:

> *Then I saw another mighty angel coming down from heaven,*
> *clothed with a cloud and a rainbow on his head.*
> *His face was like the sun, and his feet like pillars of fire.*

We know that God does appear in clouds (Job 22:14) and that clouds surround Him (Psalm 97:2), so it is not out of the question that angels would be with Him. In a vision, John saw angels flying in the sky (Revelation 14:6). And many claim to see angels in the clouds, or in cloud form. Again, secular media is reporting on the phenomenon.

Charles Shelton, a minister from West Virginia, believes he caught angels on camera. It happened when he woke suddenly with an intercessory prayer burden for his neighborhood. He told WND, "I was sent to go to the monitor. And when I went to the monitor I appeared to see the angel of the Lord coming through the wall."[46]

Meanwhile, Toby Elias spotted a cloud formation that left him speechless and recorded it on his phone. He spotted what he believes was an angel above Stonehenge. "I am unsure why religious symbols keep appearing to me—maybe I'm blessed," he told *Express*. "It was so unusual the first time around and to see an angel in the sky felt very symbolic. It feels as though someone is looking down on me."[47]

After Pope Francis was installed as the first pontiff from Latin America, people believe they saw an angel in the South Florida skies. "Most saw an angel in the clouds and grabbed their cameras to document the vision," reports WPTV.com. "For some, it was a clear sign from heaven, maybe a message from God himself, showing his pleasure at the election of the first Latin American as the 267th successor of St. Peter."[48]

Were these angels in the sky? Were these signs from heaven? Did God form the clouds to bring peace and comfort? Anything is possible, but it's more likely a random cloud formation. Scientists have recorded all manner of interesting shapes and sizes and streaks of clouds. But the fervor over angel-shaped clouds speaks to a heightened sensitivity to angelic activity in the days in which we live, even among unbelievers.

911 ANGELS REVISITED

The world will never forget when terror escalated to skyscraper proportions on September 11, 2001. And many will always remember the angelic visitations they experienced during and after the mass destruction.

Orchestrated by al Qaeda leader Osama bin Laden, nineteen men hijacked four U.S. commercial airplanes on that day. Nearly two thousand people were killed in New York City, Washington D.C., and outside a small town in Pennsylvania called Shanksville. Terrorists purposefully flew a United Airlines plane into the north and south towers of the World Trade Center site. An American Airlines plane then crashed into the Pentagon. Passengers aboard a separate United Airlines plane attempted to overthrow the hijackers. The ultimate terror target remains unknown. The plane crashed into a field, killing forty passengers and crew members.

Americans came together in that hour, crying out to God for answers and comfort. And many began reporting strong angelic activity—some of them immediately after the attacks. A former FBI employee who was on assignment at the Flight 93 crash site on September 11 says she saw a legion of angels guarding the scene. Lillie Leonardi recounted her experience in the *Shadow of a Badge: A Memoir About Flight 93, a Field of Angels, and My Spiritual Homecoming* in February 2013. Let's read her encounter in field:[49]

Angels in a Field of Tragedy

> As I looked across the immense space of the scene, I saw a shimmer of light by my left shoulder. The light flickered at first, playing against that of the sun.... On the field, the shimmer of light began to grow off to my left until it was almost blinding. I turned and looked at it more directly, and it began to evolve

into a foggy white mist. The mist then began to move, swirling in patterns of spectacular white light. Then, before my eyes, the mist took shape. To my amazement, there at the left of the crash site stood what appeared to be a legion of angels.

There were hundreds of them, standing in columns—a field of angels, emerging from the realm of the mist. I recognized them as archangels, wings arched up toward the sky. Each of them appeared to be dressed in warrior garments, like a legion of Roman centurions from centuries past. They were standing vigil, gazing at the surround perimeter. The looks on their faces were intense yet gentle. Calming. They stood like soldiers guarding their ground in preparation for the next battle. They appeared ready to receive the next command from their leader. And they clearly had a leader—for he stood majestically in front of them all.

This archangel stood with confidence, radiance, and an aura of leadership. The saber in his hand angled toward the ground in resting mode.... These celestial beings were so numerous that their features began to blend together. The pureness of their beauty—and the radiant light surrounding them—was overwhelming to me. Each was unique, and all were beautiful. I marveled at the image of these lovely creatures.

An Angel at Ground Zero

In what many are calling the "Angel of 9/11," *The Daily Mail* reported on a haunting face that appeared in a mangled girder taken from the exact spot where the first place crashed into the Twin Towers. Pictures show the face staring straight ahead with dark eyes and its mouth hanging open, as if it is screaming.

"The chilling apparition was spotted as construction workers put the finishing touches to New York's $715 million National September 11 Memorial and Museum, built to remember the 2,977 victims," *The*

Daily Mail reports. "Now many construction workers are too scared to approach the monument after the face appeared last week." "It sent people around the site running wild," one person told *The Sun* newspaper. "No one is allowed near the structure, the lighting has not been altered—it just happened by itself. We've never seen anything like it."[50]

Coincidence? Angel? Demon? Looking at the photo *The Daily Mail* provided, this does not appear to be an angel, but could represent a demon, which is a fallen angel. The mangled steel clearly shows the image of a haunted face screaming, but this is not consistent with Scriptures about angels on assignment. An angel would not be trapped in the steel and cause construction workers to flee. But demons are attracted to objects.

Just before the revival in Ephesus:

> *God worked powerful miracles by the hands of Paul. So handkerchiefs or aprons he had touched were brought to the sick, and the diseases left them, and the evil spirits went out of them.*
>
> *Then some of the itinerant Jewish exorcists invoked the name of the Lord Jesus over those who had evil spirits, saying, "We command you to come out in the name of Jesus whom Paul preaches." There were seven sons of a Jewish high priest named Sceva doing this. The evil spirit answered, "I know Jesus, and I know Paul, but who are you?" Then the man in whom the evil spirit was jumped on them, overpowered them, and prevailed against them, so that they fled from that house naked and wounded.*
>
> *This became known to all Jews and Greeks living in Ephesus. And fear fell on them all, and the name of the Lord Jesus was magnified. Many who believed came confessing and telling their deeds. Many who practiced magic brought their books together and burned them before everyone. They calculated their value, which equaled fifty thousand drachmas. So the word of the Lord powerfully grew and spread.*
>
> ACTS 19: 11–20

Were demons attracted to the magic books? I believe they are attracted to objects that represent witchcraft and the occult, such as Ouija boards. The Bible also speaks of accursed objects related to false gods in Deuteronomy 7:25–26:

> *You must burn the graven images of their gods with fire. You must not desire the silver or gold that is on them nor take any of it, lest you be snared by them, for it is an abomination to the Lord your God. You shall not bring an abomination into your house, lest you become cursed like it, but you must absolutely detest and abhor it, for it is a cursed thing.*

It's likely that the mangled steel that appeared as an angel was as symbol of the demons that inspired the hijackers to commit mass murder with a jetliner. Experts reported to NBC that the shape of the face was a manifestation of corrosion.

In another 911-related event, some reported in 2013 what they describe as the sound of angels singing coming from One World Trade Center. Some say was caused by the wind, but New Yorker Kenny Cummings called it "unmistakable and very chilling," the *Daily Mail* reports.[51]

The Sound of Angels Singing

You've probably heard the Christmas carol written by Charles Wesley, the brother of 1800s revivalist John Wesley, wherein the lyrics proclaim, "Hark the herald angels sing, 'Glory to the newborn king!'" We don't actually read about angels singing in the story of Christ's birth, but many claim to have heard angels belting out songs.

Many Christians were stunned when they heard angels singing at the Brownsville revival—and other choirs have recorded practice sessions where angels seem to have joined the chorus. In fact, WND reports a retired Air Force officer has posted an online collection of recordings of what he believes are angels singing.

"I have four specific recordings of angels singing in church settings," Jim Bramlett told WND. "It happened supernaturally. There's no other explanation. It's either from God or from the devil, and I don't think the devil is in the business of worshipping Jesus. That is not in his job description."[52]

WND also tells the story of Wayne Warmack of Greater Works Ministries in Arkansas. Warmack and his wife, Sandy, say they heard angelic voices during a Passover celebration in Florida.

> "I began to distinctly hear wordless voices in perfect harmony with us that were clearly not coming from me or Sandy, or the other 20 or so people present in the room. They sort of drifted in and out of my hearing while I struggled to maintain my composure and continue the song," says Warmack. "If you've ever heard that sound, it leaves you a different person than when you came in. I can't describe it. There's just no way to describe it. It is definitely heard with more than just the physical ears."[53]

But do angels really sing? Absolutely they do.

Job 38:7 speaks of a time "when the morning stars sang together, and all the sons of God shouted for joy." The Message version of the Bible relates, "While the morning stars sang in chorus and all the angels shouted praise." The "morning stars" in Hebrew speak of angels. The Hebrew word for "sang" in that verse means "to cry out, shout for joy, give a ringing cry, to cause to ring or sing out for joy, rejoicing," according to the *King James Old Testament Hebrew Lexicon.*

If that's not enough, Revelation 5:8–9 makes it even clearer:

> *When He had taken the scroll, the four living creatures and the twenty-four elders fell down before the Lamb, each one having a*

harp, and golden bowls full of incense, which are the prayers of saints. And they sang a new song.

ARE THESE UFOs REALLY ANGELS?

Sometimes the world doesn't know what to make of what it sees. There have been numerous articles about "unidentified flying objects," or UFOs, that some are absolutely convinced are angels.

After Donald Trump was elected president of the United States, people began reporting UFOs in the shape of an angel. Photos and videos documented what appeared to many as an angel flying through the sky over Washington, D.C. Some believe it signifies a divine blessing over Trump.[54] This is not an isolated phenomenon. A UFO shaped like an angel was also witnessed in May 2016 in the skies of Alicante in Spain.[55] In April of 2016, video emerged of an air show in Texas where a mysterious aircraft flew past a team of F-18 fight pilots at high speed.[56]

After the tragic 2016 Pulse Night Club shooting in Orlando that left forty-nine people dead and another fifty-three wounded, Corey Hearon posted a video he took on his way to work. Posted on CNN, the video shows a cloud in the shape of an angel.[57] "The wind didn't seem to disturb it, and it remained in the same place for fifteen to twenty minutes," he said in the video. "Is that not an angel or what? This is blowing my mind.... Look, you can like almost see a face. Isn't that amazing? I'm seeing an angel."

Indeed, UFO watchers are intrigued by angels and anything that manifests in the shape of an angel. But are any of the many reported UFO sightings supposed to be angels *really* angels? Most of the footage I've watched would suggest this is a stretch, but I don't doubt that there have been angel sightings in the skies. The fascination with angels among UFO hunters is telling of the pop culture phenomenon.

5

When Angels Speak and Other Controversies

It all started with an encounter. With Charles and Francis Hunter, Roland Buck told the story of what he described as "the most outstanding and thrilling thing that has every taken place in my life."[58] Of course, he is referring to angelic visitations he says he experienced over a two-year period. Buck says God clearly instructed him to share what he saw, his experiences, and messages he received from angels. The 1979 book, *Angels on Assignment,* serves this purpose. The authors write:

> God is illuminating truths of the Bible in unprecedented ways prior to the return of Jesus. Revelations are bring brought forth in all ministries flowing in the Sprit. In this relation, God quickened my spirit to John 16:12–15: "Oh, there is so much more that I want to tell you, but you can't understand it now When the Holy Spirit, who is truth, comes, he shall guide you into all truth, but will be passing on to you what he has heard. He will tell you about the future." (TLB)[59]

With the Hunters' help, Buck wrote about the many messages they received from God's angels, offering Scripture to back up what they shared. The summary of the messages was essentially, "I care!"[60] Buck didn't take the sixteen separate angelic visitations referenced in the book—each of which they say lasted two to four hours—lightly. The encounters drew them closer to God, he explained, not closer to angels. The angels, he recalls, never left without offering Bible references to where the message could be found.

Buck concluded the first chapter of *Angels on Assignment* with a friendly admonishment: "The activity of angels will intrigue you, but a word of caution was brought from God by Gabriel: "Do not seek angels. Seek Jesus! He is far greater than any angel!"[61] *Angels on Assignment* encouraged readers that angels are on assignment to help us in times of need, in line with Hebrews 1:14: "Are they not all ministering spirits sent out to minister to those who will inherit salvation?"[62]

The Man Who Talked with Angels, which included the final nine angelic visitations not offered in the first book, released in 2004. Buck's daughter, Sharon, penned the book. In 2010, Timothy Holt compiled a book called *When Angels Speak, Roland Buck on the Power of the Blood of Jesus*, which centered on the blood of Jesus. But *Angels on Assignment* continues to turn the heads and touch the hearts of many in the twenty-first century who are hungry to learn more about the heavenly host.

HERESY HUNTING OR HUNTING FOR TRUTH?

Both praise and criticism followed Buck and the Hunters in the days and years after *Angels on Assignment* pioneered the modern-day study of angelic visitations, encounters, assignments and functions. In particular, J. Rodman Williams penned a paper from the former Melodyland School of Theology in 1980 called "Angels on Assignment" to dive into what he called "widespread expression of concern about the book *Angels on Assignment*."[63]

A group of five—three professors and two regents from the school—set out to make a public declaration in two parts. First, they offered a series of biblical affirmations, warnings, and tests in relation to angelic visitations. The theologians' self-stated goal was to "make a biblical statement against which any visitations might be weighed and evaluated."[64] In other words, Scripture is the plumb line against which any experience must be judged. Second, they critiqued the book in light of their interpretation of Scripture.

The authors affirmed the following: angels are real; angels may be experienced; angels are largely anonymous; angels are little described; angels' specific roles are praising and worshipping God, announcing extraordinary events in biblical history, interpreting divine visions in biblical revelations, consoling, strengthening, protecting, delivering, giving simple directions to fulfill God's purpose, and executing judgment.

Next, the authors set forth several biblical warnings about angel encounters:

- An angel is to be accursed if he proclaims another gospel (Galatians 1:8).
- Satan disguises himself as an angel of light (2 Corinthians 11:14).
- An angel, which is a spirit, should not be believed just because it's a spirit (1 John 4:1).
- An angel could be a deceitful spirit (1 Timothy 4:1).

Finally, the authors offered five tests to judge angelic visitations in accordance with biblical commands to test the spirits (1 John 4:1) and test everything (1 Thessalonians 5:21). These five tests are:

(1) Are the angels identified by non-biblical names?
(2) Are the angels given extrabiblical descriptions?

(3) Are the angels performing roles beyond the biblical picture?
(4) Are the angels sources of additional information beyond biblical affirmation?
(5) Are the angels in any way proclaiming another gospel?

The five were especially concerned about a lack of discernment in the body of Christ, the potential for a "religion of angels" to be developed in violation of Colossians 2:18, and the danger of angels adding to the Bible in visitations (Jude 3).

PUTTING ANGELIC VISITATIONS TO THE TEST

Williams and his contemporaries citied grave concerns about *Angels on Assignment.* The first concern was that there were extrabiblical assertions in the book, such as, "No two of them look alike! They are different sizes, have different hairstyles, and have completely different appearances. Chrioni has a hairdo much like many men have today, and he looks about 25 years old."[65] A second concern involved biblical roles that go beyond the Bible, such as claims that one of the authors had engaged in fifty hours of angelic conversations in sixteen separate visitations in two years (pages 13 and 15).

The authors were also concerned about the messages the angels brought, citing chapter 6—"God's Priorities" as a key example. They rightly point out that angels in Scripture announce and interpret events, but don't offer lengthy sermons. Going deeper, the authors question Buck's description of angelic roles, such as bringing "people to a point of either accepting or rejecting Jesus."[66]

Buck, they claim, also offers angelic messages that go beyond biblical affirmation. Could it be possible, though, that angels brought further revelation on some matters in the Bible? If a doctrine is not established from such an encounter, but information is presented that sheds light on Scripture, what do we do with it? Should such revelations be kept to ourselves to prevent people from making doctrines out of the information? Is this how cults are formed?

The authors go on to dissect the book and offer strong opinions—with scriptural backup—to suggest that the book is too far beyond the bounds of Scripture to be accepted. In conclusion: Williams and his colleagues determined:

> Pastor Buck's book dramatically shows the need for firmer doctrinal understanding. At one point, in the midst of a conversation with Michael, and under Michael's influence, Pastor Buck says, "When God brings truth, we have to forget our little boxes of doctrine, for God can DO what He wants, and KNOWS what He wants to do. The critical danger here is that by forgetting our doctrine—even "our little boxes"—we may fall prey to all kinds of false doctrine: who knows, even "the doctrine of demons" (see again 1 14 Timothy 4:1). Pastor Buck's 'angels' who neither emphasize Scripture nor are much concerned about doctrine once again prove to be misleading spirits. It is fervently to be hoped that sound doctrine may again become a far more serious matter.[67]

In Buck's Defense

Still, *Angels on Assignment* was accepted by many. Nearly half a million people have visited the AngelsonAssignment.org website, and decades later, the book is still in the top 100 in Amazon's rankings of "Angelology & Demonology" books. In her book, *Revival Glory*, the late Ruth Ward Heflin, a revivalist who was widely considered a matriarch of Pentecostal faith, acknowledged the criticism of the book but also gave it high praise:

> Some folks were critical of Brother Roland Buck and his experiences with angels which he related in his book, *Angels on Assignment.* When the book was first published, Mother brought a copy with her when she visited Jerusalem. As she read it aloud to me, we cried together. We were so blessed by the stories he told. She would read a little while and we would cry a little. Then, she would read a little more and we would cry a little more.
>
> We knew that it was of God. During that time when he was getting so much criticism, somebody brought us some tapes on which he was telling the same story recounted in the book. As I listened to the tapes, I could hear the sound of eternity glory in his voice. I knew that heavenly sound. I knew that glory sound. I didn't even have to hear what he said. I recognized the realm of the Spirit. There is a glory sound that ministers to the depth of the spirit.[68]

ANGEL CONTROVERSIES RISING

Long before Buck's book was released, angel controversies were a reality in the church. Paul saw this in his day—and I believe he saw it prophetically as the Holy Spirit inspired his writing. The apostle told the church at Galatia, "Although if we or an angel from heaven preach any other gospel to you than the one we have preached to you, let him be accursed." We've seen angels preaching other gospels that have birthed false religions. We'll explore that topic more later in this chapter.

Paul also warned the church at Colossae:

> *Do not let anyone cheat you of your reward by delighting in false humility and the worship of angels, dwelling on those things which he has not seen, vainly arrogant due to his unspiritual mind, and*

> *not supporting the head, from which the entire body, nourished and knit together by joints and sinews, grows as God gives the increase.*
>
> Colossians 2:18–20

Matthew Henry, an eighteenth-century minister whose well-known commentary provides an exhaustive, verse-by-verse study of the Bible, gets to the root of such angel exaltation:

> They advanced those notions to gratify their own carnal fancy, and were fond of being thought wiser than other people. Pride is at the bottom of a great many errors and corruptions, and even of many evil practices, which have great show and appearance of humility.

In the modern church world, some are giving wild names to angels. Todd Bentley, best known for stewarding the Lakeland Outpouring until a marital affair was exposed in 2008, told the world about an encounter with an angel called Emma. This female angel, he claimed, gave him a vision of God coins that he reckoned was a sign of his prosperity. He said this female angel wore a long, white dress and floated above the floor, resembling the late healing evangelist Kathryn Kuhlman.

Rick Joyner, founder of Morningstar Ministries, set out to clarify the Emma controversy surrounding Bentley. The late prophet Bob Jones was apparently the first to report seeing this female angel. Joyner explains:

> When I asked Bob Jones about Emma, the messenger angel who has come to him on occasion to declare that there would be an outpouring of healing, Bob felt that she came in this form that was to him like a mother's compassion, which to Bob was

> the greatest compassion. The meaning of the word Emma is "whole," which is part of the revelation. In Scripture, when one was healed it was often said that they were "made whole." This, too, is obviously part of the revelation that the Lord wants us to obtain by sending a messenger about healing whose name means "whole."
>
> I have also heard it said that there is an "Emma" who seems to be what the Bible calls "an angel of light" or a false angel. That would not surprise me, but it would surprise me if there was a false angel using this name without there being a real one. The reason why there are no counterfeit $3 bills is because there are no real ones. I have never known the devil to create anything, but only counterfeit what God is doing, just as there would not be any false prophets if there were not real ones. There are also cult angels that call themselves Michael or Gabriel.
>
> I have witnessed the fruit of this angel called Emma visiting Bob Jones, and it was good and it was God, not the devil. Healing did break out; it glorified the Lord and not the devil, and it greatly encouraged and helped God's people.[69]

J. Lee Grady, former editor of *Charisma* magazine, spoke of a growing Brazilian church in Boston. The pastor there told his congregation he was having regular conversations with an angel. He wrote:

> Weeks later he set a chair on the stage for the heavenly visitor, whom he said was attending Sunday services even though no one could see him. The pastor eventually wrote a book containing messages he had supposedly received from the angel. The man's teachings became so bizarre that he was eventually removed from his denomination for promoting heresy.[70]

That scenario may seem extreme, but it is one example of widespread emphasis on angels and angelic encounters in the

> charismatic movement today. In the case of the Brazilian church, the pastor went off the theological deep end and his church became a cult. It remains to be seen what will happen in other sectors of our movement as leaders promote teachings about angels that range from the mildly weird to downright wacky.[71]

Angel controversies are nothing new and assuredly will continue to rise in the last days. Authentic and false angelic manifestations are and will become more prevalent in the last days. While we must exercise discernment, we must not let skepticism replace discerning of spirits and throw out the authentic angels with the vain imaginations.

6

Angelic Visitations Are Real

We see angels visiting men and women in the pages of the Bible—and that didn't stop after John penned the book of Revelation. God is the same yesterday, today, and forever (Hebrews 13:8). If anything, I expect these angelic encounters to increase as we move into the end times, perhaps fantastically so.

Some want to emphasize that only fifteen people in biblical history experienced angelic visitations, but Hebrews 13:2—"Do not forget to entertain strangers, for thereby some have entertained angels unknowingly"—refutes that numbering. Just as everything Jesus did while He walked the earth is not recorded in the Bible (John 21:25), it is clear that not every angelic visitation people had in the days of the Bible's penning are recorded.

Joel prophesied that in the last days God would pour out His spirit on all flesh, and that would lead to more people prophesying, dreaming dreams, and having prophetic visions, as well as witnessing wonders in the heavens (Joel 2:28–30). In other words, supernatural manifestations will increase in the end times. I believe that includes angelic visitations, and the book of Revelation backs up that assertion as angelic activity takes center stage in the last of the last days. This chapter is devoted to sharing some modern-day angelic encounters that will give you a new perspective on how angels manifest in the earth today.

AN ANGEL DELIVERS A MESSAGE OF MERCY

With hundreds of thousands of believers in America crying out for mercy in accordance with to 2 Chronicles 7:14—"If My people, who are called by My name, will humble themselves and pray, and seek My face and turn from their wicked ways, then I will hear from heaven, and will forgive their sin and will heal their land"—an angelic encounter in our nation's capital spoke hope and life in a pivotal hour.

"In February while praying at the White House, two friends and I had an angelic visitation. In response to our prayers and decrees, the angel simply said, 'Mercy, mercy, mercy, mercy, mercy, mercy.' Yes, six times," shares Dutch Sheets, an international best-selling author and conference speaker.[72] The timing was just months before the 2016 U.S. presidential election—and before President Donald Trump won the Republican nomination.

In this case, as Sheets describes the encounter, the angel appeared in human form. The angel walked toward them, then right by them as he repeated the word "mercy" six times. The angel disappeared almost as quickly as he appeared. This is a good example of an angelic manifestation, according to Hebrews 13:2 cited above. One reason we may entertain angels unknowingly is because they may appear in human form.

A HEALING ANGEL VISITS BETHEL

Bethel Redding is known around the world as a supernatural hub. Led by Bill Johnson and the birthplace of Jesus Culture, miracles, healings, and angelic visitations are reported there in far greater number than in the average church. Below is one account from Bethel of a healing angel. We see scriptural basis for a healing angel in John 5:4:

> *For an angel went down at a certain time into the pool and stirred up the water. After the stirring of the water, whoever stepped in first was healed of whatever disease he had.*

Bethel reports:

A man named Al Chadwick has been colorblind and dyslexic; he is 54. He was at work last Tuesday and felt a heavenly presence. He looked around and saw seven angels on a nearby ridge with their swords drawn. One of the angels waved at him, and he waved back. He thought, "Hey, that's kind of cool. I get to hang out with angels."

He felt a wind and looked up, but there was no wind. There was an angel standing next to him. The angel said, "You are blessed. Be healed," and touched his forehead. He noticed that there were three different shades of brown on the mountains where he was. He noticed that he could see color. He used to see differently. Yellow looked almost white. Purple didn't look quite right. He saw mostly black, white and gray and shades between.

It was difficult because when he drove through a traffic light, he had to look closely to see what was lit. He used to have trouble seeing at night. Now he can see at night, and he can see colors. God gave him a gift to release blessing on people. He told him to bless a friend, and the next day he went to his friend to pronounce blessings on him. His friend asked him about his bad dyslexia and gave him something to read. The words were perfect. He said, 'God double dipped me and I didn't even know it. God is in a good mood!' He clearly gives God the glory for his healing.[73]

A VISITATION OF WARRING ANGELS

Ché Ahn, founder of HRock Church and president and founder of HIM network, tells the story of an extraordinary angelic visitation in the Mott auditorium on May 28, 1995. His daughter, Joy, was 12 at the time and her best friend had just returned from renewal meetings at the church, full of the Holy Spirit. As Ahn tells the story, it was late when they came home, and he was trying to go to sleep when he heard laughter and banging in the family room. The girls were shaking under Holy Spirit power so hard they were thumping loudly on the floor.

Ahn asked them to quiet down and they did, but fifteen minutes later, the noise started up again. Ahn once again asked them to quiet down, and this time he didn't hear another noise. Little did he know his wife, Sue, had gone out into the living room to see what the Holy Spirit was doing with the girls, and Christine started prophesying at 1 a.m., "Mott, Mott, we've got to go to Mott."[74] Sue drove the girls to the auditorium, and the girls' eyes grew wide with awe.

> As they looked up, they began to describe seeing thousands of doves everywhere and hundreds of angels of every size and ethnic color! Sue quickly went across the street and rapped on [Lou] Engle's door. Lou came over to Mott; he, too, sensed the strong presence of the Holy Spirit, but he saw nothing. Only two little girls and Sue could see the angels and doves, along with flowers and other wonders. "It was like a scene from the book of Acts, where angelic visitations are common," Ahn explains. "They saw many other incredible things, but the most impressive to them were the angels. They described the angels as warring angels... this visitation lasted for almost six months. Other children also saw the angels at Mott."[75]

AN ANGEL ON ASSIGNMENT TO HELP

Patricia King, founder of XP Ministries, tells the story of an angelic visitation while leading a group to Tijuana, Mexico. She was commuting back and forth from Vancouver, British Colombia. While driving down Interstate 5 in California with a friend praying and fellowshipping, the car got a flat tire. The spare in the back of the car was broken, so they were stuck. King and her friend started worshipping Jesus. About five minutes later, a man pulled up in front of them and stopped.

> We didn't have any fear. We felt peace. We felt like he was a really great guy. He seemed nice and kind. And he says, "What can I do to help you?" And I said, "Well, we got a flat tire but I don't have a tire in the back that's going to work on this." And he says, "Let me see what I can do." And he went into the back of his truck and he came back with the perfect tire size, rim and everything on it. And he just pulled the whole thing off and put the new one on in no time at all.
>
> I went into the vehicle to get my bag. I wanted to give him a gift and go back and thank him. And I went to say goodbye and thank you and give him this gift. I'd only been gone for a few seconds. He was gone, nowhere to be seen. We didn't know what happened to him or the truck. And I believe that it was an angelic visitation.[76]

AN ANGELIC ARMY OF WAR

During the late 1940s and early 1950s, well-known evangelist Ernest Angsley baptized people in Spring Creek, the original settlement of Rosehead, which later became Perry, Florida. Today, Jim Rawlins, founder of Keys of Awakening Ministries, says angels are encamped there:

> On April 11, 2015 we gathered on the banks of Spring Creek, at its head, for a time of worship. As the people worshipped, suddenly I began to be drawn to the far side of the spring. As I walked around the spring I sensed the presence of an encampment of thousands of angels. I never saw any of them but knew they were present and were simply sitting or standing around.[77]
>
> As I walked through the encampment one spoke to me saying, "We have been waiting for generations. Where have you been?" After returning to the people on the south side of the spring I asked my wife to walk around the spring with me, not telling her what to expect. As we approached the north side, she also sensed the presence of angels. It is quite interesting that one section of Folsom Park was named for a young lady who was killed in a car wreck. Her name was Angel and the dog park is named "Angel's Dog Park."[78]

Rawlins is convinced that this was a confirmation of a prophetic word released by Ken Malone, founder of Forerunner Ministries, who had given these words to his church on January 30, 2015:

> I will leave a mark of redemption and healing in Perry. I have assembled an angelic army for war and harvest. I will awaken a sleeping giant called the church that shall begin to possess the land and atmosphere of this region. The Big Bend will bend in worship and humility for three days. I say to "Occupy" the territory through worship for three days and I will release My Presence in the land. Prepare, prepare, prepare for in these three days you will possess the land.[79]

ANGELS THAT ASSIST WITH MIRACLES

After an experience of being caught up into heaven, Pastor Gary Oates, author of *Open My Eyes Lord*, started seeing angels while ministering to people. Sid Roth summarized Oates' experience, which happened while he was on a trip with Randy Clark in Brazil, based on his radio broadcast:

> After I took off my shoes, my eyes were opened and I was astonished by the sight of three angels worshipping God through dance! They seemed transparent; I could see right through them—and they wore white flowing robes. Above the speaker's platform was an even more amazing sight—angels singing and playing musical instruments! The indescribable beauty of all this engulfed and overwhelmed me. I raised my hands to Heaven, and as tears ran down my cheeks, I prayed, "Oh God, I want more of you!"
>
> As I worshipped God and cried out for more of Him, I began to feel myself growing taller, until I could look down and see everyone in the tent. My spirit continued to ascend, and I could see over the whole city. I cannot fully describe the sensation, but I felt that nothing was impossible, and realized that there were no limitations in the Spirit. Then I saw Jesus coming down, holding His hands out to me. He held my hands tight and said, "I will not let you go." My left hand, where Jesus held it, began to burn and felt like it was on fire.
>
> After a long while in which I experienced many things, He let go of my hands, and I began to descend back to the meeting. My spirit came back into my body with such force that I was thrown backward through the chairs. It was noisy and startled the people around me, but to me it felt like landing in a bed of feathers. I felt like I was nailed to the floor, and I could not move

for about an hour. As I lay there, I basked in the beautiful, glorious presence of God. When I finally stood up, all I could do was cry and stagger around. I even had to have help walking.

As Gary allowed God to cleanse him, he began to discern the presence of angels. He could literally see them healing people and driving out demons. Randy Clark asked him to pray for the sick, and a long line formed. When he prayed, he saw huge warrior angels put their wings around people; every person he prayed for was healed.

In one case, Gary prayed for a man with advanced brain cancer. Gary said that he saw an angel blowing fire from his mouth like a blowtorch, onto the man's head. He asked the man what he was experiencing, and the man said, "My head feels like it is burning up and on fire." Then the man raised his hands and shouted "I'm healed. I know I'm healed!" Gary encouraged him to go back to his doctor and get a medical verification of his healing, even though the man said he did not need it. After being healed, the man and his wife received salvation. Gary believes that healing is a very powerful tool for evangelism.

Gary also said that another man came to the platform for healing and the power of God hit him, knocking him down. The man later shared this: "God took me into his presence and I saw two large chains holding a chest full of sins and burdens. The chains were cut, and I felt free and liberated, then angels washed me. After being washed, I was taken back into the presence of God, and given this message:

> **Wake up! Wake up! Many in my church are sleeping. Many go through the motions but few have entered into intimacy with me. What I desire you have above all**

things is an intimate relationship with me. The quicker you enter into this relationship the quicker the world will be won, and I will come and take you home."

As Gary reflects on his experiences, he says that he has continued to see angels and to witness miracles, healings, signs and wonders as part of his every day experience, but that no one should think this is meant for him, alone. God desires this level of intimacy with everyone. The average believer can move in this power. This is God's desire for us. Gary says that what we must do is allow the Holy Spirit to move in our lives and make us clean in order to be able to see into the supernatural.[80]

ANGELS GUARDING A GENERATION

In his book, *Angel Armies: Releasing the Warriors of Heaven*, Tim Sheets tells the story of ministering at a church in Jacksonville. He arrived late, but when he walked in he sensed God's supernatural activity was stirring in the worship service.

> As I walked from the back to the front of the auditorium, I began to see flashes of light going back and forth across the congregation. I stopped I my tracks because, as I have taught, that refers to angelic activity. Angels were moving all around the auditorium, ministering to God's people.... The next morning began as the worship leader opened with a song to gather everyone together and prepare their minds for receiving mode. My brother, Dutch Sheets, opened the service in prayer. I stood there on the front row, getting ready to minister, when I saw, off to the right, a group of angels. To the left there was a group of

> angels stationed as well. They were angel warriors. I looked up and saw angel warriors stationed everywhere.[81]

This, of course, was enough to capture his attention, but even more so because something similar had happened a few months before in New York. Sheets reports seeing two bands of angels on each side of those who had been called to the altar after Cindy Jacobs called teenagers and adults up to the age of 30 up for prayer:

> While we were praying, I heard, called out from behind me, "Mahanaim." I know exactly what Mahanaim is because I teach about it. Of course, God knew that word would grab my attention and I would recognize it meant the Angel of the Lord who accompanies the apostolic assignment on my life. Finally I looked to see who was yelling, "Mahanaim." To my surprise, there was nobody behind me. I began to shake internally.

Mahanaim is a Hebrew word found in Genesis 32. Jacob left Laban to return home and was going to meet his brother Esau, whose birthright he stole. Scripture records Jacob witnessing two groups of angels protecting his family. Jacob called that place *Mahanaim*, which means "the place of two camps," according to Strong's Concordance.

> Back to the meeting in Jacksonville: I remembered what I had seen in New York and what I read in Genesis 28. I saw the same thing and knew the Holy Spirit was using the angels to protect what He is doing with the coming generation—particularly that night, what He was doing with the youth in that church.... I have now had two encounters with Mahanaim, seeing them surround, as guards, the next generation.[82]

Warning: Not All Angelic Visitations Are Real

Although angels can visit, we have to fall back on the Bible to judge supernatural experiences. Second Timothy 3:16–17 tells us:

> *All Scripture is inspired by God and is profitable for teaching, for reproof, for correction, and for instruction in righteousness that the man of God may be complete, thoroughly equipped for every good work.*

At the end of the day, we must maintain our focus on the God of the angels rather than on the angels themselves. If we obsess over angelic visitations, we will find ourselves out of balance and open a door for the enemy to bring deception to our minds. I don't see anywhere in Scripture where people fervently seek out angelic visitations.

We cannot decide to have an angelic visitation any more than we can decide to have a spectacular vision. God may choose to send an angel to offer direction, but angels should not replace the leadership of the Holy Spirit in our lives. When we put more emphasis on angels than we do on the Father, Son, and Holy Spirit, we're ripe for deadly error. Indeed, entire religions have been founded based on revelations from angels. Cults have risen up based on one man or woman's experience with an angel.

Islam Founded on False Angelic Revelation

A man named Muhammed, who claimed to be a prophet, founded Islam in 610. PBS reports:

> According to Muslim belief, at the age of 40, Muhammad is visited by the angel Gabriel while on retreat in a cave near Mecca.

> The angel recites to him the first revelations of the Quran and informs him that he is God's prophet. Later, Muhammad is told to call his people to the worship of the one God, but they react with hostility and begin to persecute him and his followers.[83]

Encyclopedia Brittanica continues:

> The archangel Gabriel brought the Qur'ān down to the Prophet's "heart."[84] Gabriel is represented by the Qurān as a spirit whom the Prophet could sometimes see and hear. According to early traditions, the Prophet's revelations occurred in a state of trance when his normal consciousness was transformed. This state was accompanied by heavy sweating. The Qurān itself makes it clear that the revelations brought with them a sense of extraordinary weight: "If we were to send this Qurān down on a mountain, you would see it split asunder out of fear of God.[85]

Muslims do not believe in the deity or the crucifixion of Jesus Christ. Muslims believe Jesus was fully man and a respect Him as a prophet, but not the Son of God. This flies in the face of Scripture. Yet, Islam is the fastest-growing religion in the world—and, again, it was birthed from a false angelic visitation. Whether or not Mohammed made up the story or an angel of light visited him, we do not know.

MORMON CHURCH ARISES FROM DEMON VISITATION

The Church of Jesus Christ of Latter-Day Saints, known as Mormonism, is based on a visitation from an angel of light. Joseph Smith, founder of Mormonism, left record of the 1823 encounter, which is chronicled on the religion's website, LDS.org:

On the evening of September 21, [Smith] determined to ask forgiveness for his sins and follies so that he might know his standing before God. Of that night in 1823, Joseph wrote, "I had full confidence in obtaining a divine manifestation, as I previously had one…A personage appeared in Joseph's bedroom, surrounded by brilliant light: 'His whole person was glorious beyond description, and his countenance truly like lightning.'"

This glorious being introduced himself as Moroni, stating that he was a messenger sent from the presence of God. He said that God had a work for Joseph to perform, and then he prophesied that Joseph's name would be "had for good and evil" among all peoples of the earth. (JS—H 1:33.) The heavenly visitor then spoke of the book that Isaiah had seen in a vision, explaining that it contained an account of this continent's former inhabitants, and it also contained "the fulness of the everlasting Gospel" as delivered by the Savior to those ancient peoples. He told Joseph of the Urim and Thummim, which had been prepared to help in translating the record. (JS—H 1:34–35.) Moroni also quoted many passages of scripture relative to the establishment of this dispensation and the great changes it would bring on the earth. (JS—H 1:36–41.)

Oliver Cowdery recorded that while Moroni was speaking, a vision was also opened to Joseph's mind, so that he was permitted to see marvelous manifestations relative to what was being taught. (Latter Day Saints' Messenger and Advocate, Kirtland, Ohio, Apr. 1835, p. 112.) Concluding his presentation, Moroni warned Joseph that when the time came to obtain the plates, if he showed them to anyone not approved of the Lord, he would be destroyed. The light gathered around the heavenly messenger, a conduit opened up into heaven, and Moroni ascended. (See JS—H 1:43.) Moroni's visit to Joseph Smith was repeated twice more that night, and Moroni gave the same message and added warnings, including one that Joseph must resist the temptation to use the plates to make himself and his family rich.[86]

Smith wrote:

> The fundamental principles of our religion are…concerning Jesus Christ that He died was buried, and rose again the third day, and ascended into heaven; all other things which pertain to our religion are only appendages to it.[87]

But Mormons also believe *The Book of Mormon, Doctrines and Covenants*, and *The Pearl of Great Price* are divinely inspired. They believe Father God was not always God, that He was not the Creator but was Himself created. Mormons believe there are levels of heaven we attain based on works. Mormons believe Jesus was birthed through a physical relationship between God the Father and Mary. All of this defies Scripture.

After early persecution, this false religion propagated like wildfire. Today, the Church of Jesus Christ of Latter-Day Saints reports a total membership of 15,882,417 million in 30,304 congregations around the world. The Book of Mormon has been published in 188 languages. The church has 70,946 missionaries in the field, 15 missionary training centers and 155 temples.[88]

In more recent years, Jose Luis de Jesus Miranda, a heretic with a 666 tattoo who claimed to be the Messiah, says he discovered he was Christ after angels visited him in a dream. CNNreported his key messages: There is no devil and no sin and we can do no wrong in God's mind.[89] At the same time, false messiahs are rising around the world. As legitimate angelic encounters increase, it's important to remember as we open our eyes to the reality of angels that no angel replaces the Holy Spirit or contradicts the Word of God.

7

Discerning the Presence of Angels

If you are like most people—if you are like me—you've never actually seen an angel. You've never had an angelic encounter or a visitation—but you know that angels are all around you (Psalm 34:7). You know that the heavenly host is warring for the will of God. You know angels are harkening the voice of God's word (Psalm 103). You know that angels can manifest as people, and it's possible that you have encountered an angel in human form.

If you are like me, you may have even sensed the presence of angels by your spirit even though you did not see them with your natural eyes. When it comes to the angelic realm, we can train our senses to discern angelic activity—and it's important that we do so we can cooperate with the work the Lord has sent them to do in our midst.

The Bible says, "But solid food belongs to those who are mature, for those who through practice have powers of discernment that are trained to distinguish good from evil" (Hebrews 5:14). Many in the body of Christ have trained their senses to discern evil spirits. In the same way, however, we can train our senses to discern the Holy Spirit and His ministering spirits—the angels sent to minister to the heirs of salvation.

WHAT DISCERNMENT IS AND IS NOT

Discernment. All Christians need it, but some haven't taken the time to cultivate it. Discernment is absolutely vital in prophetic ministry. There are two angles to explore: the gift of discerning of spirits and discernment. One is a gift. The other is developed. But even if you have the gift, you still need to cultivate it. The Bible is full of warnings about deception and it cautions us to discern.

> *For such are false apostles, deceitful workers, transforming themselves into apostles of Christ. And no wonder! For Satan himself transforms himself into an angel of light.*
>
> 2 CORINTHIANS 11:13–14

> *But there were also false prophets among the people, even as there will be false teachers among you, who will secretly bring in destructive heresies, even denying the Lord who bought them, and bring on themselves swift destruction. And many will follow their destructive ways, because of whom the way of truth will be blasphemed. By covetousness they will exploit you with deceptive words; for a long time their judgment has not been idle, and their destruction does not slumber.*
>
> 2 PETER 2:1–3

> *For false christs and false prophets will rise and show great signs and wonders to deceive, if possible, even the elect.*
>
> MATTHEW 24:24

Of course, it's not just devils we need to discern. We need to discern God's presence. We need to discern the human spirit. We need to discern who—and who not—to enter relationships with. We need to discern what to do with our finances. We need to discern God's will for our lives. There is no "book of Jennifer" in the Bible to tell me what to do. I have to discern God's will, and so do you. We need to hunger for discernment. Even people who walk closely with God and hear His voice accurately can massively miss it.

Discernment is "the quality of being able to grasp and comprehend what is obscure," also "an act of perceiving or discerning something," according to *Merriam-Webster*. Discerning means "able to see and understand people, things, or situations clearly and intelligently."

The Vine's Complete Expository Dictionary of Old and New Testament Words reveals that the words "discern," "discerner," and "discernment" come from several Greek words. *Anakrino* means "to distinguish, or separate out so as to investigate by looking throughout objects or particulars," hence it signifies "to examine, scrutinize, question, to hold a preliminary judicial examination preceding the trial proper." *Diakrino* signifies "to separate, discriminate;" then, "to learn by discriminating, to determine, decide." *Dokiamazo* signifies "to test, prove, scrutinize;" so as "to decide."

John tells us to test the spirits to see if they are from God (1 John 4:1). We can't see spirits—whether demons or angels—unless the Lord opens our eyes. But we should look with our spiritual eyes to discern the spiritual activity around us. Second Corinthians 4:18–19 says "we do not look at the things which are seen, but at the things which are not seen. For the things which are seen are temporal, but the things which are not seen are eternal." We need to be heavenly minded with an eternal view even while we walk the earth in our physical bodies.

Developing Our Spiritual Senses

Discerning the presence of angels requires us to develop our spiritual senses—to train our spiritual eyes and spiritual ears to see and hear what the Lord and His angels are doing and saying. When Jesus said, "He who has ears to hear, let him be listening and let him consider and perceive and comprehend by hearing" (Matthew 11:15), He was speaking of spiritual ears and spiritual discernment. He was speaking of matters not revealed by flesh and blood, but revelation from the Spirit of God.

Remember, you are a spirit, you have a soul, and you live in a body. We don't touch or receive the things of the kingdom with our physical bodies and natural senses. We touch and receive the things of the kingdom of God with our spirit man and spiritual senses. In his letter to the church at Corinth, Paul the apostle writes:

> *For the Spirit searches all things, yes, the deep things of God. For what man knows the things of a man, except the spirit of man which is in him? Likewise, no one knows the things of God, except the Spirit of God. Now we have received not the spirit of the world, but the Spirit which is of God, so that we might know the things that are freely given to us by God. These things also we proclaim, not in the words which man's wisdom teaches, but which the Holy Spirit teaches, comparing spiritual things with spiritual. But the natural man does not receive the things of the Spirit of God, for they are foolishness to him; nor can he know them, because they are spiritually discerned.*
>
> 1 Corinthians 2:10–14

We don't discern the deep things of God—including the presence of angels—with our mind. And it's important to note that angels don't appear unless God wants them to. We discern angels by the Spirit of

God bearing witness with our spirit man. The Spirit of God within us helps us discern spiritual things. You might say it's not by wisdom or by reasoning but by the Holy Spirit's teaching.

That's not to say that our physical senses are never involved in discerning angels, but they are discerned primarily through the spiritual senses—even if we see them through our natural eyes or have physical contact with them, as Daniel did in his encounters. There may also be times when we notice something with our natural senses first, then discern it by the spirit. We need to enroll in the School of the Spirit and lean on the Word of God to train our spirits to see the things of the kingdom of God, including His angels.

How Our Natural Senses Come into Play

Against that backdrop, let's look at how God can use our natural senses to alert us to spiritual things—including the presence of angels. Our natural, or physical senses are hearing, seeing, tasting, smelling, and touching. We'll briefly examine each natural sense from a spiritual point of view.

Hearing: I can hear the voice of God through people, songs, television broadcasts, and so on. What I mean by that is that God causes something to stand out, or even jolt my hearing. In these cases, it's as if what is being said demands my attention. It could be a confirmation of something the Lord has said to me previously, it could be a key phrase that spurs me to prayer, or it could be the sound of wind, rain, or just about any noise that could resonate with my spirit man.

In Luke 24, some disciples encountered Jesus but did not recognize Him as the Lord. After the revelation that He was the risen Christ, they asked: "Did not our hearts burn within us while He talked to us on the way and while He opened the Scriptures to us?" (Luke 24:32). In this passage, we see their hearts were hearing something beyond what their natural ears heard, but their natural ears were the gateway to their spiritual ears.

Seeing: I have seen glory clouds and demons. I've had visions from God. I have not seen an angel, but many do see angels with their physical eyes as well as with their spiritual eyes. When God opens our eyes, it may be in the form of a prophetic dream, a vision, a trance, or even what feels like a real-life experience in heaven or hell.

Although we should not seek a supernatural experience for its own sake, we should seek God and trust that He will give us what we need. Nothing is wrong with crying out to God to open our eyes when we sense that we aren't seeing what He really wants us to see.

In Elisha's day, the king of Syria was warring against Israel. The prophet Elisha gave the Israelites a marked advantage—he was able to hear the words Syria's king spoke in his bedroom and relayed them to the king of Israel (2 Kings 6:12). The Syrian king wanted Elisha stopped, and sent out horses and chariots and a great army to fetch him. When he saw the Syrian army surrounding the city, Elisha's servant got scared:

> *And his servant said to him, "Alas, my master! What shall we do?" So he answered, "Do not fear, for those who are with us are more than those who are with them." And Elisha prayed, and said, "Lord, I pray, open his eyes that he may see." Then the Lord opened the eyes of the young man, and he saw. And behold, the mountain was full of horses and chariots of fire all around Elisha.*
>
> VV. 15–17

Tasting: The Bible tells us to "taste and see that the Lord is good" (Psalm 34:8). The Hebrew word for taste in that verse is *ta'am,* which means "to taste, perceive, eat." Sometimes, things we taste as spiritual tip-offs aren't so pleasant. We may taste bitterness when someone around us has a bitter spirit. We know that both John and Ezekiel ate scrolls that tasted like honey in their mouths, but afterward, they were bitter in their bellies (Ezekiel 2:8; Ezekiel 3:3; Revelation 10:9–10).

Smelling: I've experienced smells of smoke, which can often point to demons in our midst. I've also smelled the fragrance of God, which I can best describe as the scent of flowers. Deep worship, abandonment, and surrender—a willingness to yield to His every movement as we listen for the sound of His heart—ushers us into the Holy Spirit's presence in a magnificent way. Sometimes we can even smell His fragrance.

In Song of Solomon, the Shulamite woman declares that God's love is better than wine: "Because of the fragrance of your good ointments, Your name is ointment poured forth" (Song 1:3–4). Where the name of Jesus is exalted in adoration, the stage is set to enter into a secret place in which we smell that anointed ointment that's poured forth in our midst.

Touching: Many times the Lord will speak to us through physical sensations in our body, almost like sympathy pains when a man's wife is pregnant. Some people get tingling skin or burning eyes. Many people can feel the presence of the Lord and can in a similar way sense the presence of angels. I've known people who can feel angels touching them. We know an angel struck Peter on his side (Acts 12:7)—and I'm sure he felt that!

Five Ways to Cultivate a Discerning Spirit

Discernment is a vital gift in an age when false apostles, deceitful workers, demonic angels of light, false signs and wonders, false prophets, false teachers, false christs, false revivalists, and other falsities are rising in the church.

Some believers have the gift of discerning of spirits, but every believer can develop a discerning spirit. Indeed, we need to hunger for discernment in this hour, because signs and wonders will mark the next great move of God, but the enemy will come in—as the Bible warns in 2 Corinthians 11:13–14, 2 Peter 2:1–3, Matthew 24:24, and other places—with deceptions and counterfeit anointings at the same time.

Even people who walk closely with God and hear His voice accurately can massively miss it. The Gibeonites tricked Joshua into making a covenant with them, and he ended up having to go to war to defend them. The Bible says he "did not ask counsel of the Lord" (Joshua 9:14). A young prophet didn't discern an old prophet lying to him and paid for it with his life (1 Kings 13:1–24). Even Samuel, a prophet whose words never fell to the ground, missed it by relying on his natural eyes. He thought surely Eliab was God's choice to replace Saul (1 Samuel 16:6–13).

We need discernment in the spiritual realm, but we also need discernment to navigate the many decisions in our life. We need to know the will of the Lord. Discernment is not a feeling, it's a knowing. If we have a feeling, we must not act until the feeling is a knowing. Our emotions will betray our discernment. We need to see with our spirit and not our soul. So how do we get discernment? Here are five ways.

1. Ask for discernment.

Like wisdom, discernment flows out of a fear of the Lord and we can ask for it. James 1:5 says

> *If any of you lacks wisdom, let him ask of God, who gives to all liberally and without reproach, and it will be given to him.*

We could put "discernment" in that verse and it would still ring true. Matthew 7:7–8 promises:

> *Ask, and it will be given to you; seek, and you will find; knock, and it will be opened to you. For everyone who asks receives, and he who seeks finds, and to him who knocks it will be opened.*

And remember Solomon, who asked for:

...an understanding heart to judge Your people,
that I may discern between good and evil.

1 KINGS 3:9

God wants us to have discernment. He wants us to be wise regarding the manifestation of spiritual gifts and decisions about our lives. If we need discernment, we must ask for it. In Paul's apostolic prayer, he prays, "that the eyes of your understanding may be enlightened" (Ephesians 1:18). We can ask God for discernment—to open our spiritual eyes. But we don't need to just ask for it in the moment we need it. We need to ask for it regularly.

2. Seek godly counsel.

Remember, our emotions can betray us. We should seek counsel from those who are more experienced in life or more discerning than we are. Personally, I always seek counsel from various perspectives when I face a problem or need to make an important decision. I hear the voice of the Lord in good counsel. Proverbs 11:14 tells us:

Where there is no counsel, the people fall;
But in the multitude of counselors there is safety.

And Proverbs 15:22 says:

Without counsel, plans go awry, But in the multitude
of counselors they are established.

We can sharpen our own skills by listening to good counsel.

3. Stay in the Word.

The Word of God gives us God's perspective on all matters of life. The book of Proverbs, in particular, is an excellent tool for strengthening our discernment. When we need discernment, we should pray and ask the Lord—then go to His Word. We should always judge our discernment against the Word of God.

Hebrews 4:12 tells us:

> *For the word of God is living and powerful, and sharper than any two-edged sword, piercing even to the division of soul and spirit, and of joints and marrow, and is a discerner of the thoughts and intents of the heart.*

And Romans 12:2 warns:

> *Do not be conformed to this world, but be transformed by the renewal of your mind, that by testing you may discern what is the will of God, what is good and acceptable and perfect.*

If we know the Word—and we know the character of God by studying His Word—we will cultivate discernment. Anything that does not line up with God's Word does not come from God, because the Spirit and the Word agree (1 John 5:8).

4. Exercise discernment.

In a biblical warning of apostasy, Hebrews 5:11–14 says:

> *Concerning this we have much to say that is hard to explain, since you have become hard of hearing. For though by now you should be teachers, you need someone to teach you again the first principles*

of the oracles of God and have come to need milk rather than solid food. Everyone who lives on milk is unskilled in the word of righteousness, for he is a baby. But solid food belongs to those who are mature, for those who through practice have powers of discernment that are trained to distinguish good from evil.

We need to be open-minded, but, as it's been said, we don't need to be so open-minded that our brains fall out. When we meet new people, we should use discernment. The Bible says to know people by their fruits (Matthew 7:16).

5. Don't go by what you see with the natural eyes alone.

Remember, Joshua and Samuel both went by what they saw or heard. Paul, by contrast, didn't let what he saw or heard move him. When the damsel with the spirit of divination followed Paul and Silas around, declaring that "these men are servants of the Most High God, who proclaim to us the way of salvation" (Acts 16:16), Paul waited to discern what was happening.

On the surface, the girl spoke facts. But the Bible says she did this for many days. Paul was greatly troubled in his spirit—he discerned something was wrong. Finally, he turned to the spirit and told it to come out in the name of Jesus. Paul illustrated what John 7:24 admonishes us to do:

Do not judge according to appearance, but judge with righteous judgment.

8

Why Angelic Visitations Will Rise in the Days Ahead

The numbers of angelic visitations are rising and will continue to increase in the days ahead—and the awareness of the angelic realm is contributing to that spike. Put another way, angelic encounters are rising, but with the increased understanding of angelic ministry through books, television programs, and newspaper reports, the increased numbers of angelic visitations are being documented and educating the masses—both believers and unbelievers—that angels are real and active.

"In these days, we will see the manifestation of the power of God escalate in the earth. Just like Jesus, the company of those who perform His miraculous works will increase," says Patricia King, founder of XP Ministries. "Visions will increase. Angelic visitations will increase."[90]

Mike Bickle, director of IHOPKC in Kansas City, believes many things will begin happen as a result of this outpouring of the Spirit mentioned in Joel 2:28:

> *And it will be that, afterwards, I will pour out My Spirit on all flesh; then your sons and your daughters will prophesy, your old men will dream dreams, and your young men will see visions.*

Visions of angels are included in this prophetic realm. Bickle says:

> It will have so many multi-dimensional expressions that it cannot be simply an evangelism movement, a healing movement, a prayer movement, a unity movement or a prophetic movement. Above all things, it will impart and renew deep, affectionate passion for Jesus through the Holy Spirit. The increase of prophetic ministry in the local church involves more than verbal, inspirational prophecy. In my understanding, it includes angelic visitations, dreams, visions, and signs and wonders in the sky, as well as an increase in prophetic revelation, even the kind given through subtle impressions of the Holy Spirit.[91]

Reputable leaders across the body of Christ agree we should expect angelic activity to increase in the days ahead. The big question is why? We see a relative handful of angelic encounters—including dreams and visions of angels—in the Bible, so what's driving what appears to be an exponential increase in the occurrence of angelic activity in modern times?

In my research and interviews with many who have had angelic encounters in line with Scripture, I have received varied answers to the "why" question. However, there is a running theme—a string that holds together the many perspectives. It seems that as the hour draws ever-closer to the Second Coming of Christ, angels are preparing people for His return. Some of the ways we believe this preparation comes is in the form of angel armies, angelic intervention, angels of God's presence, and angels bringing in the harvest.

God Is Releasing Angel Armies in This Hour

Tim Sheets, author of *Angel Armies*, says angelic activity will now increase dramatically. He has seen an uptick of angelic activity in his own life, and has completed a comprehensive study of angels over the past decade. He says:

> Angels assist Holy Spirit and the heirs of salvation (Hebrews 1:14) to do God's will upon the earth. They work to enforce the decrees of God's Word (Psalm 103:20). We are living in the season of the greatest move of God in history. Angels are needed to help facilitate that move.
>
> Also, the Word of God is now being released in faith decrees as never before. Millions of them. This is activating angels to assist Holy Spirit to bring them to pass. In 2007 as Holy Spirit began to download a revelation concerning angel armies. He spoke this to me, "The greatest days in church history are not in your past, they are in your present and your future." To see those days increased angel activity is a must.[92]

We Should Expect Miraculous Angelic Intervention

Jeff Jansen, founder of Global Fire Ministries, reminds us that angels have always been part of the communication process with God from the foundation of the world—and we would be hard pressed to not find a place in both the New and Old Testaments where angels were not active in the lives of men and women as God was moving with His people.

As a matter of fact, he says, Scripture is filled with accounts of angels on assignment in the lives of the patriarchs in helping to establish the Kingdom of heaven in their midst. Jansen says as it was then so it is now.

> We should always expect miraculous intervention from heaven in our lives. The key word is "expect." To the degree that we look with eyes of faith to expect and see the supernatural in our lives, will be the degree that we will actually see it manifest. Angels are part of God's Kingdom economy. They are part of the Kingdom of God. Bob Jones told me once that the only credit that angels get in heaven comes from how they successfully work with us.[93]

Jansen relies on Scripture to back up his point. The Bible says without faith it is impossible to please God. When we exercise faith, he says, the angels are released, and, according to Psalm 103:20, they "do His mighty works of power." As we speak and move in faith, he says, they ride on the currency of the power of the spoken word to perform the word of the Lord.

> When we prophecy, decree, speak kingdom words they are released to accomplish and fulfill that word or decree of power. So we should always speak in faith, always prophecy and decree, and as we do angels will be released and supernatural influence and power will be released and executed in and around us. This is why it is so important for us to be careful what we speak. Life and death are in the power of the tongue. Proverbs 18.[94]

ANGELS OF HIS PRESENCE MANIFESTING IN MANY WAYS

James Goll, author of *Angelic Encounters: Engaging Help from Heaven*, says we shouldn't just expect angelic visitations to increase in the near future—we should expect it now. Like his contemporaries, he already sees an increase of angelic activity in the earth today.

Goll says:

> Angels of His presence is one of the primary categories of angels that have and are being released. That is part of the reason why there is such an increase of the manifested presence of God in our worship services. Yes, this tangible presence of God is a dimension of the Holy Spirit. But in many places there is another level that is already upon us. His presence is intensifying because we are drawing Angels themselves to come and join in with us in our worship and praise.[95]

Goll describes the manifestation of angelic visitation in several ways. One is an atmosphere "getting thicker." Another is increased anointings. Yet another is spontaneous healings happening as we extravagantly enter worship and praise. That, he says, is because angels are worshipping with us, but they are also ministering to us. That is part of their job description, according to Hebrews 1:17 and 24.

> *Do you feel the fire of His presence increasing? Do you feel an actual wind blowing? Are healings happening without anyone laying hands on anyone? If that is the case, then the Heavenly Host has just joined you, we, and they are releasing the Kingdom of God in our midst. In His Kingdom there is His rule and reign. The King sits and He reigns. We then experience a heightened awareness*

of angelic activity and a super charged atmosphere of faith where all things are possible.[96]

ANGELS BRINGING IN THE HARVEST

Matt Sorger, author and founder of Matt Sorger Ministries, says the angelic is an integral part of what God is releasing in these days. He stresses that angels are ministering spirits sent on assignment to minister to the heirs of salvation and believes angels not only minister to the saved, but are also being used by God to bring in the harvest.

"Angels help break demonic strongholds over regions so that region can experience the freedom and liberty of Christ," Sorger says. "There is a rise in intercession occurring. As God gives clear discernment, effective intercession will break the influence principalities and powers have held over territories.

"With this breakthrough," he continues, "I believe we will see an increase in salvations as well as an increase in notable miracles and the display of God's power. There will be a greater manifest flow of God's presence in the church and as a result a greater outflow through the church."

As Sorger sees it, we are in a season of harvest with a greater manifestation of God's power in the works of Christ. He sees angels are on assignment as the church prophecies, decrees and releases the word over people, region,s and cities.

"Angels are preparing the way for a fresh anointing to hit God's people in an astounding way. I believe angels are also being sent on assignment to release the fire of God that will set many free from besetting sin and old cycles of the flesh," Sorger says. "A new wave of freedom and deliverance will be released on mass and God will mobilize His angels to help in this."

9

Angelic Activity as a Sign of the End Times

The Bible has plenty to say about the signs of the times—that is, the marking of the end times. Many believe the escalation of angelic activity is one of them.

Matthew 24 outlines many of the signs of the times we reference. The passage is too long to pour out here, but some highlights are worth noting: Many will come in Jesus' name claiming to be the Christ and will deceive many (Matthew 24:5). We're seeing a rise in the number of people claiming to be Christ right now, and there will be more to come. There will be wars and rumor of wars, and nations will rise against nations and kingdoms against kingdoms (Matthew 24:6–7). There will be famines, epidemics, and earthquakes in various places (Matthew 24:7).

We're seeing all of this as well, and although it's not new, there seems to be an uptick in such activity. Jesus said, though, that this would only be the beginning of sorrows.

He prophesied about the increase in persecution against believers (Matthew 24:9–10). He also warned about the great falling away of believers, which will include betrayal (Matthew 24:10). Next, comes the rise of false prophets who deceive people and love growing cold (Matthew 24:11–12). Jesus told His disciples when they see the abomination of desolation, they should flee because a great tribulation will follow (Matthew 24:15–21). Jesus went on to mention false prophets and false christs deceiving people a second time (Matthew 24:26).

Jesus made it clear that no one—not even the angels in heaven—knows the day or the hour of His Second Coming (Matthew 24:36). He admonished His disciples to watch, pray, and be faithful and wise servants because He will come back when we least expect it.

What the Bible Says About the End Times

Before we get into speculation and sightings of end-times signs, let's look at what the Bible says about the last of the last-days signs:

> *Know this: In the last days perilous times will come. Men will be lovers of themselves, lovers of money, boastful, proud, blasphemers, disobedient to parents, unthankful, unholy, without natural affection, trucebreakers, slanderers, unrestrained, fierce, despisers of those who are good, traitors, reckless, conceited, lovers of pleasures more than lovers of God, having a form of godliness, but denying its power. Turn away from such people.*
>
> 2 TIMOTHY 3:1–5

> *Now the Spirit clearly says that in the last times some will depart from the faith and pay attention to seducing spirits and doctrines of devils, speaking lies in hypocrisy, having their consciences seared with a hot iron, forbidding to marry, and commanding to abstain from foods, which God has created to be received with thanksgiving by those who believe and know the truth. For*

everything created by God is good, and not to be refused if it is received with thanksgiving, for it is sanctified by the word of God and prayer.

1 TIMOTHY 4:1–5

Know this first, that there shall come scoffers in the last days who walk after their own lusts, and say, "Where is the promise of His coming? For since the fathers fell asleep, all things have continued as they were since the beginning of the creation."

2 PETER 3:3–4

Concerning the times and the seasons, brothers, you have no need that I write to you. For you know perfectly that the day of the Lord will come like a thief in the night. When they say, "Peace and safety!" then sudden destruction will come upon them as labor upon a woman with child, and they shall not escape.

1 THESSALONIANS 5:1–3

But the day of the Lord will come like a thief in the night, in which the heavens will pass away with a loud noise, and the elements will be destroyed with intense heat. The earth also and the works that are in it will be burned up.

2 PETER 2:10

EXPLORING THE SIGNS IN THE SKY

Most of the signs of the times have to do with the behavior of people, with warnings that we should watch and pray, and with manifestations in the earth. But there are also signs in the sky. Jesus summed up His Matthew 24 answer to the disciples who were questioning the signs of the end of the age this way:

Immediately after the tribulation of those days, "the sun will be darkened, the moon will not give its light; the stars will fall from heaven, and the powers of the heavens will be shaken." Then the sign of the Son of Man will appear in heaven, and then all the tribes of the earth will mourn, and they will see the Son of Man coming on the clouds of heaven with power and great glory. And He will send His angels with a great sound of a trumpet, and they shall gather His elect from the four winds, from one end of the heavens to the other.

Matthew 24:29–31

And Joel prophesied:

And it will be that, afterwards, I will pour out My Spirit on all flesh; then your sons and your daughters will prophesy, your old men will dream dreams, and your young men will see visions. Even on the menservants and maidservants in those days I will pour out My Spirit. Then I will work wonders in the heavens and the earth—blood and fire and columns of smoke. The sun will be turned to darkness, and the moon to blood, before the great and awe-inspiring day of the Lord comes.

Joel 2:28–31

The Rise of "Sky Trumpets"

One phenomenon we've been hearing about in recent years is trumpets in the sky. Are these hoaxes or legitimate signs? I'll outline a few of the instances here and let you decide for yourself. Either way, the hubbub over these sky trumpets—even the mainstream media has reported on the events—reveals an interest among some and an obsession among others about the angels on assignments blowing trumpets, as we read in the book of Revelation.

The Daily Mail reports:

> A mysterious noise from the sky is continuing to baffle people all over the world—as well as giving those who hear it sleepless nights. Sounding like a trumpet or a collective from a brass section of an orchestra, a selection of videos shot from the Canada to Ukraine, via the U.S., Germany and Belarus show strange goings on above us. And the eerie sounds have been continuously heard at all different times and locations for almost a decade.[97]

According to the report, some speculate that the sounds are tectonic plates grinding, atmospheric pressure, or trains. Others believe the sounds in the sky are construction noise, UFOs, or the U.S. government using secret weapons for defense purposes or to modify the weather. Still others are certain it's a sign of the apocalypse and the seven trumpets of heaven. *Breaking Israel News* offers a Jewish perspective of these sounds, noting that the shofar sound will mark the final arrival of the Messiah.[98]

In November 2016, *The Sun* reported on a sound heard around the world that some called an "apocalyptic noise"[99] after Donald Trump's election as president of the United States. Video footage shows the rising sun in Serbia accompanied by a loud noise. Many believe it was merely a military drill, especially since the sound was heard again a few days later. But others insist this was the first four trumpets of the Revelation.

Beyond the end-times signs, the Bible does point to a trumpet blast at the presence of the Lord. Exodus 19:16 reads:

> *So on the third day, in the morning, there was thunder and lightning, and a thick cloud on the mountain, and the sound of an exceedingly loud trumpet. All the people who were in the camp trembled.*

Verse 19 tells us that sound grows louder and louder. "Many people throughout the world today have the sense that we may indeed be approaching the final period of the present age,"[100] end-times expert and author Joel Richardson told WND. He continued:

> Given that reality, it's interesting that these unexplainable sounds bear a peculiar resemblance to the sound of trumpets. The Scriptures, of course, tell us that it is at the final trumpet that Jesus will return to overthrow this present wicked system, and establish his kingdom here on the earth. One could also say that it sounds as if the earth itself is groaning under the burden of bearing the increasing sins of mankind. So also do the Scriptures tell us that all of creation itself is groaning and yearning for the return of Jesus.[101]

ANGELIC SIGNS IN THE SKY?

Videos on YouTube claim to show the angel of the Lord appearing in Arizona.[102] Other videos show what many called the fourth horseman of the apocalypse during MSNBC coverage of riots in Egypt in 2011.[103] A green horseman was also seen in a photograph circulating the Internet. The green rider reportedly appeared in the skies of Nottingham in Britain, but it was part of a scientific project called Nimbus from the University of Leeds.[104]

From New York to Hawaii, WND reported "spectacular images" of the sun and published some images that looked angels, doves, and crosses. These images went viral on Facebook, but not everyone was convinced it was a supernatural manifestation.[105] Yet another video points to what looks like a massive pentagram that started a discussion around end-times prophecy being fulfilled before our eyes.[106]

Of course, most have heard about the blood moons and the black moons. Again, there is lots of speculation, and no one can prove these signs are from God. But it demonstrates a fascination with angels, demons, and the supernatural as we draw closer to the Second Coming.

10

How Angels Operate in the End-Times Drama

Read the book of Revelation and you enter an end-times drama full of spectacular angelic encounters, prophetic announcements, and horrifying judgments. Indeed, for all the angelic activity in the Old Testament, the end times will see a dramatic surge in the occurrence of angels on assignment for the Lord. Although we're not living in the scenario described in the book of Revelation yet, we are in the last days, and we're edging ever closer to the drama John recorded that will eventually unfold with angels playing a starring role in the cast.

The book of Revelation opens with mention of an angel to present apocalyptic visions to John the apostle (Revelation 1:1). Revelation speaks of seven stars, which are the seven angels of the seven churches to which Jesus writes His letters of praise and correction

(Revelation 1:20). After John scribed these weighty letters under the inspiration of the Holy Spirit, he saw a "strong angel" proclaiming with a loud voice, "Who is worthy to open the scroll and to break its seals?" (Revelation 5:2).

Notice that the end-times angels are strong and loud. John's visions shows the angels saying with a loud voice:

> *Worthy is the Lamb who was slain, to receive power and riches and wisdom and strength and honor and glory and blessing.*
>
> REVELATION 5:12

John saw an angel ascending from the east—holding the seal of God—who cried out with a loud voice to the four angels to whom God gave power to bring harm to the earth and the sea (Revelation 7:2). He saw seven angels who stand before God receiving seven trumpets (Revelation 8:2), an angel with a golden censor standing at the altar in front of God's throne (Revelation 8:3), and the smoke of incense with the saints' prayers rising before God from the angel's hand (Revelation 8:4). In a dramatic episode, that same angel took the censer, filled it with fire from the altar, and poured it in the earth, resulting in thunder, lightning, and earthquakes (Revelation 8:5).

ANGELS BLOWING TRUMPETS THAT RELEASE HORROR

The drama only escalates from there, with the seven angels getting ready to sound the trumpets God gave them (Revelation 8:6). The angels of God are on assignment to execute the judgment of God.

When the first angel blows his trumpet, hail and fire mixed with blood will fall on the earth, and a third of the trees and grass will be set ablaze (Revelation 8:7). The second angel will blow his trumpet, and what John described as a huge, flaming mountain will be thrown into the sea, turning it into blood (Revelation 8:8). When the third angel blows his trumpet, a burning star falls from heaven and into a third of the rivers and springs, making them bitter and causing a wave of death (Revelation 8:10–11).

If the angelic theatrics ended there, it would be overwhelming enough—but that's not even half of it. When the fourth angel blows his trumpet, a third of the sun, moon, and stars go dark, bringing great darkness on the earth (Romans 8:12). Imagine what went through John's mind as he saw an angel flying across heaven shouting, "Woe, woe, woe to the inhabitants of the earth, because of the other trumpet blasts of the three angels, who are yet to sound!" (Revelation 8:13).

When the fifth angel blows his trumpet, a star falls from heaven to earth with the key to the bottomless pit (Revelation 9:1). The angel of the bottomless pit, called Apollyon, will arise before the sixth angel blows his trumpet, and the four angels bound at the Euphrates River are released to kill a third of all mankind (Revelation 9:11–15). Suddenly, an angel clothed in clouds with a rainbow on his head, a face like the sun, and feet like fire comes down from heaven with a little scroll and stands on the sea and on the earth, lifting up his hand to heaven (Revelation 10:5).

I can't fathom standing in John's shoes when a voice from heaven tells him to take the little scroll from the angel's hand or when the angel tells him to eat the scroll, which is sweet like honey in his mouth, but sour in his belly (Revelation 10:8–10).

With great anticipation over the seventh trumpet, an angel charges John with measuring the temple of God and the altar and the worshippers inside before the Two Witnesses are sent to prophesy in sackcloth for 260 days (Revelation 11:1–3). Finally, "The seventh angel sounded, and there were loud voices in heaven, saying: 'The kingdoms of the world have become the kingdoms of our Lord, and of His Christ, and He shall reign forever and ever'" (Revelation 11:15).

The Angels Warring, Preaching, Warning, and Reaping

After the seventh trumpet, a war breaks out in the heavens. The archangel Michael and his angels enter battle against the dragon—Satan himself—and the accuser of the brethren is cast down (Revelation 12:7–10). What a mighty victory this is, and it paves the way for something we've never seen in our days—angels preaching the gospel:

> *Then I saw another angel flying in the midst of heaven, having the eternal gospel to preach to those who dwell on the earth, to every nation and tribe and tongue and people. He said with a loud voice, "Fear God and give Him glory, for the hour of His judgment has come. Worship Him who made heaven and earth, the sea and the springs of water."*
>
> REVELATION 14:6–7

Angels announce the fall of Babylon (Revelation 14:8) and warn against taking the mark of the beast (Revelation 14:9) and reaping a harvest in the earth (Revelation 14:15–19).

Angels Releasing the Last Plagues and a Glimpse of Heaven

If the results of the angels blowing trumpets are frightening, the angels assigned to pour out the last plagues from bowls they carry is bloodcurdling. John describes the scenario:

> *After this I looked. And now the temple of the tabernacle of the testimony in heaven was opened. The seven angels came out of the temple with the seven plagues. They were clothed in pure, bright*

> *linen, having their chests wrapped with golden sashes. Then one of the four living creatures gave to the seven angels seven golden bowls full of the wrath of God, who lives forever and ever.*
>
> REVELATION 15:5–7

Beginning in Revelation 16, we see the angels pouring out the seven bowls of God's wrath. Nasty sores inflict those who have the mark of the beast. The sea becomes like blood and everything in the sea dies, followed by the rivers and springs turning into blood before the sun grows so hot that it burns mankind. Angels pour wrath on the beast's throne and fill his kingdom with darkness, causing them to chew their tongues because of the pain. The Euphrates River dries up, and finally wrath is poured into the air.

Angels on assignment with God's judgment then turn to "the great prostitute who sits on many waters, with whom the kings of the earth committed adultery, and the inhabitants of the earth were made drunk with the wine of her sexual immorality" (Revelation 17:1–2). Revelation 18 chronicles the angels working to bring down Babylon on orders from God before Revelation 19 shows us how angels announce the Supper of the Lamb. Revelation 20 makes believers shout, as an angel is sent on assignment to bind Satan and cast him into the bottomless pit for one thousand years. In Revelation 21, the scene shifts, and we see twelve angels standing at twelve gates in heaven, and we get a glimpse of heaven.

FALLEN ANGELS RISING IN THE END TIMES

Just as God's angels are taking on new assignments in the end-times drama, the book of Revelation also chronicles demonic assignments in the last hours. Indeed, fallen angels are also on assignment. Although there is debate about the interpretation of some of these passages about fallen angels—just as there is about the entire book of Revelation and the Second Coming of Christ—it is worth noting the parallel increase in demonic activity in the last days as revealed in John's final book.

In line with what Daniel prophesied as the seventieth week in Daniel 9:24–27, the battle between good and evil starts in the second three and one-half years of the seven-year period of the last days. Daniel calls this "the time, times, and half a time," and it marks the beginning of the Great Tribulation. The scene is set in Revelation 12:7–12, which was referenced above:

> *Then war broke out in heaven. Michael and his angels fought against the dragon, and the dragon and his angels fought, but they did not prevail, nor was there a place for them in heaven any longer. The great dragon was cast out, that ancient serpent called the Devil and Satan, who deceives the whole world. He was cast down to the earth, and his angels were cast down with him.*
>
> *Then I heard a loud voice in heaven, saying: "Now the salvation and the power and the kingdom of our God and the authority of His Christ have come, for the accuser of our brothers, who accused them before our God day and night, has been cast down. They overcame him by the blood of the Lamb and by the word of their testimony, and they loved not their lives unto the death. Therefore rejoice, O heavens, and you who dwell in them! Woe unto the inhabitants of the earth and the sea! For the devil has come down to you in great wrath, because he knows that his time is short."*

This one spoken of is described as Apollyon, who is king over the bottomless pit, in Revelation 9:11. We see the rise of persecution against the people of God Revelation 12:13–16:

> *When the dragon saw that he was cast down to the earth, he persecuted the woman who gave birth to the male Child. The*

woman was given two wings of a great eagle, that she might fly into the wilderness to her place, where she is to be nourished for a time and times and half a time, from the presence of the serpent. Then the serpent spewed water out of his mouth like a flood after the woman, that he might cause her to be carried away by the flood. But the earth helped the woman. The earth opened its mouth and swallowed the flood which the dragon spewed out of his mouth. Then the dragon was angry with the woman, and he went to wage war with the remnant of her offspring, who keep the commandments of God and have the testimony of Jesus Christ.

Satan organizes the forces of hell to rise against the coming King. Put another way, Satan builds a kingdom on earth. We read about this in Revelation 13:1–4:

I stood on the sand of the sea. And I saw a beast rising out of the sea, having seven heads and ten horns, with ten crowns on his horns, and blasphemous names on his heads. The beast which I saw was like a leopard. His feet were like those of a bear, and his mouth like the mouth of a lion. The dragon gave him his power and his throne and great authority. I saw one of his heads as if it was mortally wounded, but his deadly wound was healed, and the whole world marveled and followed the beast. They worshipped the dragon who gave authority to the beast. And they worshipped the beast, saying, "Who is like the beast? Who is able to wage war with him?"

And again we see persecution rising against God's people in Revelation 13:5–7:

He was given a mouth speaking great things and blasphemies. And he was given authority to wage war for forty-two months. He opened his mouth to speak blasphemies against God, to blaspheme

His name and His tabernacle and those who dwell in heaven. It was granted to him to wage war with the saints and to overcome them. And authority was given him over every tribe and tongue and nation.

Satan continues working to erect his kingdom and steal as many souls as possible in Revelation 13:11–17:

Then I saw another beast rising out of the earth. He had two horns like a lamb and he spoke like a dragon. He exercises all the authority of the first beast in his presence and causes the earth and those who dwell on it to worship the first beast, whose deadly wound was healed. He performs great signs, making fire come down from heaven on the earth in the sight of men. He deceives those who dwell on the earth by the signs which he was granted to do in the presence of the beast, telling those who dwell on the earth to make an image to the beast who was wounded by a sword and lived. He was allowed to give breath to the image of the beast, that the image of the beast should both speak and cause as many as would not worship the image of the beast to be killed. He causes all, both small and great, both rich and poor, both free and slave, to receive a mark on their right hand or on their forehead, so that no one may buy or sell, except he who has the mark or the name of the beast or the number of his name.

Demons continue manifesting at various points when the trumpets blow until he is finally defeated. The enemy's fate is the lake of fire. Jesus speaks of this in Matthew 25:41:

Then He will say to those at the left hand, "Depart from Me, you cursed, into the eternal fire, prepared for the devil and his angels."

II

What Angels Are Speaking Now

By all accounts and testimonies, angelic appearances around the world have increased in recent years. Even if half of the accounts are imaginary or even fabricated, the rise of angelic activity among respected voices in the body of Christ is noteworthy. So since angels are appearing, intervening, and delivering messages around the world, what are they conveying? Is there a theme to what they are communicating? I interviewed key leaders in the body of Christ who have had experiences with angels to get some insight.

"Angels are communicating strategies for the greatest campaign in church history. The theme is 'harvest, harvest, harvest.' This includes awakening and revival," says Tim Sheets, author of *Angel Armies*. "Holy Spirit is releasing angels in unprecedented numbers to do as on the Day of Pentecost in Acts 2—fire up the Remnant to be His witness. He is releasing them to communicate the message of heaven through apostolic and prophetic hubs. Part of this theme is that it is time to be the supernatural church of His presence—the glorious church—and reap a billion-soul harvest as He has prophesied."[107]

Jeff Jansen, founder of Global Fire Ministries, says angels are conveying the word of the Lord for particular cities, regions, and nations as well as the word of the Lord globally. But there is a common theme: the soon return of Jesus Christ. Jansen says:

> According to Psalm 104:4 and Hebrews 1:4, referring to the angels, He makes His messenger winds and His ministers flames of fire. Angels are both winds and flames, winds being messenger and flames meaning healing power and might. They work with us as we deliver the message. They reinforce the reality of the Kingdom of power and glory worldwide.

James Goll, author of *Angelic Encounters: Engaging Help from Heaven*, rattled off a list of instructions the heavenly host of angels is declaring in this hour: breakthrough, prepare, be on the alert, go forth, the time to shift from reformation to transformation, a call for the shields of the earth to arise to protect Israel, and a time of great harvest upon us.

"I actually had an angel come and appear at the end of my bed, wake me up and declare, 'Be on the alert!'" Goll says. "My senses were heightened and I knew that sudden change was coming across the face of the earth. Prophetic evangelists are being selected and empowered and the heavenly host are engaged in this process."

Matt Sorger, author and founder of Matt Sorger Ministries, agrees, but hears angels at the same time heralding consecration and purity. Consecration and purity prepare the hearts of God's people to move in signs, wonders, and miracles that will cause the lost to see that Jesus is alive. Sorger states:

> As angels are fighting on behalf of God's people they are helping many overcome temptation and sin and live in a deeper level of consecration. With this consecration is coming a greater glory and empowerment. A new greater authority will be displayed

in and through the church. I know Christ is coming again, but I also know it's for a glorious bride without spot or wrinkle. I believe God is calling many to a fresh consecration, to remove any landing place the enemy could have in their lives."

Angels Speak about the Second Coming

Next question: Are more angels speaking about the Second Coming of Jesus Christ? Sheets answers with a resounding "yes." He told me that a common theme of angels is "no more delay":

> Behold, He is coming quickly. Angels are helping with the message of urgency. But it is more my experience that they are doing this for the most part by preparing the way for His return. They are involved in helping to accelerate Kingdom of God activity on earth, which will hasten His return. Before Christ returns a massive harvest must be reaped. Angels are working that with urgency. I believe the angel armies will become even more aggressive as the ekklesia begins to mature, meaning those who rule and reign with Christ's authority.

Jansen reminds us that angels have different functions. His experience is that most of them do not speak, but rather come to reinforce what the Holy Spirit is doing in a particular meeting in a particular area:

> Some bring works of power, others are messenger angels that will bring messages through dreams, visions and even audible form. In seasons of transition angels are particularly active in communicating directives from the Lord. Remember they are servants sent out in the service of those who are to inherit salvation. Their job is to assist us as we administrate Kingdom authority and

function. Communication angels such as Gabriel bring national words about new seasons and transitions.

From Goll's perspective, the angelic host is speaking the word "prepare." He believes heaven's emphasis is on a great harvest. Some would contend that that means the Second Coming is imminent, but he believes we must not look for an escape hatch of deliverance from the world in this period. He notes:

> If we adopt that view, we could actually be postponing His soon and sudden appearing versus helping to "hasten the day." In the past, we have missed some of our divine opportunities because we were teaching a misapplication to a prophetic word or even one spoken via an angel.

Goll stresses that we cannot afford to be walking in presumption and thus end up in misinterpretation and wrong applications. If we keep our focus clear on the Great Commission, he says, ultimately this leads into the Second Great Coming of the Lord Jesus Christ. But if we put our emphasis in a wrong manner on the Second Coming as our way out of this mess, he says, we will have acted in a counterproductive manner to God's intention.

USHERING IN AN END-TIMES AWAKENING

Could God use angels to usher in another Great Awakening before the return of Christ? If so, how? Sheets is seeing five distinct divisions of angels the Holy Spirit is now releasing to assist the New Testament Church. First, he says, there are angels who are helping minister a fresh new Pentecost: a new outpouring. Second, there are angels who are ministering to build Kingdom government, a ruling and reigning *ekklesia*.

Sheets says Kingdom of God government will now increase, greatly assisted by these powerful angels. He continues:

> Third, angels of healing and miracles are being released. Dramatic and visual healings and miracles will now go to new levels. Holy Spirit is opening healing wells and angels are assisting that movement. Fourth, angels of evangelism are now being released. They have three areas they are primarily targeting: Prodigals—millions of prodigals will return to Christ, new converts are being drawn in and true five-fold ministry evangelists are being connected to apostolic hubs to fuel regional revival. These angels will help usher in a Great Awakening.

Just as angels were active and highly used in the First Coming of Jesus Christ, angels will also be active and highly used in His Second Coming. Jansen points to how Gabriel came to Zechariah in Luke 1:17 and announced that the aging man would have a son named John who would move in the spirit and power of Elijah, and God would use Him to turn people back to Him.

"Elijah's job was to turn Gods people's hearts back to Him," Jansen says. "In 1 Kings 18:7, Elijah said 'How long will you be between to opinions, if Baal is god serve him, but if God is God serve Him,' and he backed up his ministry with fire from heaven to consume the sacrifice.

"The people's hearts were tuned back to God—that's revival. Angels are always involved in the transition and establishing of the new. So it will be in this great glory revival as we are now in the beginning stages before the return of Christ. Angelic activity and revelation are increasing that are a precursor for awakening."

Sorger believes angels are sent on assignment as we prophecy, decree, and declare God's Word and take authority over the works of darkness. He sees that regions that have been hindered by principalities and powers will experience great breakthrough, and he predicts a resurgence of God's manifest presence where before it has been "hard" in the spirit.

"As angels help clear out the spiritual atmosphere, God's house will be filled with a greater weight of glory," Sorger says. "As a result, there will be more salvations, healings, breakthrough and deliverance. I believe we will see a rise in strategic, anointed and discerning intercession that really hits the target. Great freedom and release will come to many. We will see mass deliverance released as the atmosphere shifts and God's glory crashes in breaking and demolishing strongholds that have held people captive."

Goll says he saw these words written in large, amber glowing letters before his eyes: "The Beginning of the third Great Awakening!" "When I move into the 'seer realm,' it often comes with angelic assistance, he says. "This is something I have learned over my many years of prophetic ministry. When that realm opens up to me in eternal visions and the manifested presence becomes every so thick, it is in part due to angels on assignment."

Releasing Anointings to Believers

Beyond all of this, many agree angels are releasing anointings that believers need in this hour. Sorger believes angels will help usher in the manifest fire of God, bringing cleansing and freedom. He points to Isaiah 6:6–7, which shows how angels can help minister cleansing and purging. He calls out Acts 5:19, Psalm 34:7 and Acts 12:7, which show how angels can help bring breakthrough and deliverance. He experienced this in a meeting in England, when God sent a seraphim angel. I'll let him tell the story:

> During the morning service I was worshipping God. Suddenly I began to feel a heat radiating from my left side. I stretched out

my hand into the empty space of air next to me and found the air was hot in that one place. I thought to myself, "There's a pillar of fire standing next to me!" Then God spoke to me and said He had sent a seraphim angel into the meeting. I had a different teaching planned for that morning, but God just took the service over.

That night when we returned to the church, I found my entire body getting hot about an hour before the meeting. When we came into the church the temperature was comfortable. As the meeting progressed it became so hot in the room the ushers had to open all the windows and doors. People began to take every extra layer of clothing off that they could. That seraphim angel was in the room and the tangible fire of God was being poured out.

When I stood to the podium to speak, God struck me mute. I couldn't talk for two hours. As I stood there staring at the people, the fire of God swept through the place like the coal that touched Isaiah's lips in Isaiah 6. A holy fire from God swept over the people and many were cleansed and gloriously set free. The tangible presence of God became so intense some people ran out of the church into the streets crying out, "The fire of God is in the church!" This fiery angel was sent on assignment from God to release a holy fire and commissioning to God's people.

With all the talk of a generational shift—the aging Baby Boomers, the passing of the torch to Generation X and the rising Millennial generation, Sheets sees angels that assist a transgenerational effort by Christ's Kingdom.

"These angels help the generations synergies together," Sheets says. "They are helping Holy Spirit release a transgenerational anointing that will empower us to see the greatest days in church history. We need the coming generation and I believe angels are assisting us with that right now."

12

Activating Angels on Assignment

Biblical scholars can argue whether angelic activity is increasing in this hour, but prophetic voices insist that angels are on assignment with increasing intensity. As heirs of salvation, we must understand the many functions of angels and cooperate with the Lord and His angels to see His good, perfect, and acceptable will come to pass in our lives.

Speaking of angels, the Bible says:

> *Are they not all ministering spirits sent out to minister to those who will inherit salvation?*
>
> Hebrews 1:14

From this verse, we see the apostolic nature of angels—God sends them on ministry assignments to help us. God ultimately chooses if and when to send angels, but we can release activation prayers that set the stage for God to respond with angels.

In the realm of angelic revelation, we must take caution to remain balanced. First Peter 5:8 (AMPC) offers a clear warning:

> *Be well balanced (temperate, sober of mind), be vigilant and cautious at all times; for that enemy of yours, the devil, roams around like a lion roaring in fierce hunger, seeking someone to seize upon and devour.*

Just as there are many believers who reject the notion that an angel can appear with a message, assist in healing ministry, or execute some other assignment for the Lord, there are others who put too much emphasis on angels—and still others who make up encounters with strangely named angels that don't exist.

JESUS IS SUPERIOR TO ANGELS

We must remember that Jesus is superior to the angels. The writer of Hebrews rightly pointed out in Hebrews 1:5–13:

> *For to which of the angels did He at any time say: "You are My Son; today I have become Your Father"? Or again, "I will be a Father to Him, and He shall be a Son to Me"? And again, when He brings the firstborn into the world, He says "Let all the angels of God worship Him."*
>
> *Of the angels He says: "He makes His angels spirits, and His servants a flame of fire." But to the Son He says: "Your throne, O God, lasts forever and ever; a scepter of righteousness is the scepter of Your kingdom. You have loved righteousness and hated wickedness; therefore God, Your God, has anointed You with the oil of gladness more than Your companions."*
>
> *And, You, Lord, laid the foundation of the earth in the*

> *beginning, and the heavens are the works of Your hands. They will perish, but You remain; and they all will wear out like a garment; as a cloak . You will fold them up, and they will be changed.*
>
> *But You are the same, and Your years will not end. But to which of the angels did He at any time say: "Sit at My right hand, until I make Your enemies Your footstool?"*

Acknowledge God in All Your Ways

Even—and especially—in the context of angel activations, it's vital we don't displace Father, Son, and Holy Spirit in our lives. The Father sent Jesus to pay the price for our sins and pave the way to salvation. Jesus sent the Holy Spirit.

Jesus told His disciples:

> *But the [a] Helper (Comforter, Advocate, Intercessor—Counselor, Strengthener, Standby), the Holy Spirit, whom the Father will send in My name [in My place, to represent Me and act on My behalf], He will teach you all things. And He will help you remember everything that I have told you.*
>
> John 14:26, AMPS

Jesus has the preeminence in our lives. He can choose to dispatch angels, but the choice is His. The Bible admonishes us to acknowledge God in all our ways and He will direct our paths (see Proverbs 3:6). It doesn't say to acknowledge angels in all our ways. The Bible says to seek first the kingdom of God and His righteousness, and everything we need will be added to us (see Matthew 6:33). It doesn't say to seek first angels.

There are different times, reasons, and seasons to activate specific angels on assignment in our lives. I believe the Holy Spirit gives us an unction or a leading to activate those angels by praying His Word and declaring His will. When we're sensitive to the Holy Spirit's voice, we will discern the unction to release angels to act.

As we move through the angel activations in the coming chapters, we must be careful not to give glory to angels that belongs only to God; be careful not to exalt angels to a place that belongs only to Jesus; and avoid relying on angels when we should be depending on the Holy Spirit.

Remember, angels obey the Lord—not man:

Bless the Lord, you His angels, who are mighty,
and do His commands,
and obey the voice of His word.

PSALM 103:20

13

ACTIVATING ANGELS OF PROMISE

From Hagar to Elijah, God sends angels on assignment to deliver a promise key times in the lives of men and women in Scripture. In fact, the very first time we find the word "angel" in Scripture, we have a promise in a wilderness place.

In Genesis 16, we read the account of an angel of the Lord. Jehovah cut a covenant with Abraham and told him his descendants would be as innumerable as the stars. The only problem was Sarai, Abram's wife, could not bear children. As we often do in our impatience and with our finite minds that can't quite understand that God can do the impossible, Sarai decided to "help the Lord along" in manifesting this profound prophetic word.

Sarai told Abram to have intimate relations with her maid, Hagar, so that she could bear children for him. Abram took Hagar as a second wife and she conceived. Problems started when Hagar started despising Sarai, who in turn grew angry with Abram. Abram effectively told his wife to handle Hagar herself.

Then Sarai dealt harshly with her, and she fled from her presence. The angel of the Lord found her by a spring of water in the wilderness. It was the spring on the way to Shur. And he said, "Hagar, Sarai's maid, where have you come from and where are you going?" And she said, "I am fleeing from the presence of my mistress Sarai." Then the angel of the Lord said to her, "Return to your mistress, and submit yourself to her authority." The angel of the Lord also said to her, "I will multiply your descendants exceedingly so that they will be too many to count."

GENESIS 16:6–10

You may be in a wilderness place right now. You may have been thrust into a situation that you didn't expect, despised and rejected by people who should have defended you, and otherwise expelled from a community that should embrace you. If so, you can ask the Lord to send an angel on assignment with one of God's seven thousand-plus promises to strengthen your heart to endure the desert.

When you find yourself in a wilderness place waiting on the promise of God to manifest—whether that's a Scripture you're standing on or a prophetic word you are warning according to 1 Timothy 1:18—God may lead you to activate angels of promise.

Angelic Activation Prayer

Father, I thank you that my wilderness experience has not escaped you. I trust in You in this desert place. I'm grateful for your many promises and for your Holy Spirit, who leads and guides me into all truth. Father, in the name of Jesus, activate your angels of promise in my life to meet me in the midst of this trial and deliver a message of promise in my pain, just as you did for Hagar. Holy Spirit, comfort me and show me things to come.

14

Activating Angels of Warning

While the Holy Spirit warns us of impending danger, God can send angels on assignment to warn us of situations and circumstances we need to avoid and even show us the way of escape. Such was the case in the hours before the destruction of Sodom and Gomorrah.

Picture the scene: Two angels came into the wicked city. Lot was there at the gate and insisted they stay the night at his home. The angels followed him home—and so did the wicked men of the city who insisted Lot open the door so they could "have relations" with them. As the account goes, the angels struck the immoral men blind (see Genesis 19:1–10).

> *Then the men said to Lot, "Have you anyone else here? Sons-in-law, sons, daughters, or anyone you have in the city, take them out of this place! For we are about to destroy this place, because the outcry against its people has grown great before the presence of the Lord, and the Lord has sent us to destroy it."*

So Lot went out and spoke to his sons-in-law, who had married his daughters, and said, "Get up, get out of this place, for the Lord will destroy this city!" But to his sons-in-law he seemed to be joking. When the morning dawned, the angels urged Lot, saying, "Arise, take your wife and your two daughters who are here. Otherwise you will be consumed in the punishment of the city."

GENESIS 19:12–15

Angels can also appear in our dreams carrying warning messages. Joseph, Jesus' earthly father, experienced one on more than one occasion. Let's explore these accounts to build our faith.

Now when they departed, the angel of the Lord appeared to Joseph in a dream, saying, "Arise, take the young Child and His mother, and escape to Egypt, and stay there until I bring you word. For Herod will seek the young Child to kill Him."

MATTHEW 2:13–14

And again…

But when Herod was dead, an angel of the Lord appeared in a dream to Joseph in Egypt, saying, "Arise, take the young Child and His mother, and go into the land of Israel, for those who sought the young Child's life are dead."

MATTHEW 2:19–20

God can send angels on assignment with words of warning. Those who heed the angelic warning will find deliverance from danger. Those who ignore the urgent pleas of angels could face dire consequences. Lot's sons-in-law did not escape the wrath of God. The Lord rained fire and brimstone on Sodom and Gomorrah and overthrew the cities and all the people remaining in them.

Angels offer extremely strong warnings in the end-times drama, before the ultimate rise of the Antichrist and the Second Coming of the Lord. We see this in Revelation 14:9–10:

> *A third angel followed them, saying with a loud voice, "If anyone worships the beast and his image and receives his mark on his forehead or on his hand, he also shall drink of the wine of the wrath of God, which is poured out in full strength into the cup of His anger. He shall be tormented with fire and brimstone in the presence of the holy angels and in the presence of the Lamb."*

Ultimately, the Holy Spirit shows us things to come—including warnings. He gives us checks in our spirit. We may have dreams and visions exposing the enemy's plans. We may receive a prophetic word from a human messenger from God. But it's just as Scriptural for God to send an angel to warn us of impending danger, either while we are awake or while we are asleep.

The Holy Spirit may lead you to activate angels of warning by allowing you to sense His urgency about situations or events at hand for those for whom you are making intercession. You may not hear His voice, per se, but you may sense that He is trying to give you a heads-up about an enemy attack around the corner against you or someone you care about.

When you've prayed in the Spirit and in your natural language, and you still have no understanding of what He is saying, you can ask the Holy Spirit to warn and protect the person. You can also pray to activate angels to warn the person even when—and especially when—you cannot reach them yourselves.

Angelic Activation Prayer

Father, I thank you that the Holy Spirit speaks to my heart, but sometimes I miss that still, small voice in my spirit. I thank You that the steps of a righteous man are ordered of the Lord, but I know sometimes I misstep and move out of your grace in my folly. I ask you in those times to show mercy and send angels on assignment with a warning so I can avoid destructive situations in my life.

In Jesus' name.

15

Activating Angels of Provision

From Hagar to Elijah, we see angels of provision in Scripture. It's been said God is not late, but He rarely shows up early. When God sends angels on assignment with provision, they are always on time.

In Genesis 21, we see the ongoing drama between Hagar and Sarai, now called Sarah. Sarah had given birth to the child of promise, Isaac. Hagar's son, Ishmael, was mocking Isaac—and Sarah got angry. She told Abraham to cast Hagar and Ishmael out of the camp. This was distressing for Abraham, but he obliged.

> *So Abraham rose up early in the morning, and took bread and a skin of water and gave it to Hagar, putting it on her shoulder, and sent her away with the child. So she departed and wandered in the Wilderness of Beersheba.*
>
> *When the water in the skin was gone, she placed the child under one of the shrubs. Then she went and sat down across from him at a distance of about a bowshot, for she said to herself, "Let*

> *me not see the death of the child." She sat across from him, and lifted up her voice and wept.*
>
> *And God heard the boy's voice. Then the angel of God called to Hagar out of heaven and said to her, "What is the matter with you, Hagar? Do not be afraid, for God has heard the voice of the boy where he is. Arise, pick up the boy and hold him in your hands, for I will make him a great nation." Then God opened her eyes, and she saw a well of water. And she went and filled the skin with water and gave the boy a drink.*
>
> GENESIS 21:14–19

The angel of provision reminded her of what the angel of promise had said. Were these two angels one and the same? We don't know, but we do know that the angel reminded Hagar of the promise and pointed her to provision.

We also see angels of provision visiting Elijah after his battle with the false prophets on Mount Carmel. Jezebel sent a messenger of fear with a death threat, and Elijah went running into a cave in the wilderness. We read the account in 1 Kings 19:4–8:

> *He went a day's journey into the wilderness and came and sat down under a juniper tree and asked that he might die, saying, "It is enough! Now, O Lord, take my life, for I am not better than my fathers." As he lay and slept under the juniper tree, an angel touched him and said to him, "Arise and eat." He looked, and there was a cake baked on coals and a jar of water at his head. And he ate and drank and then lay down again. The angel of the Lord came again a second time and touched him and said, "Arise and eat, because the journey is too great for you." He arose and ate and drank and went in the strength of that food forty days and forty nights to Horeb, the mountain of God.*

God can send angels on assignment with provision for you. That doesn't mean that we should wax lazy and depend on angelic provision, but it does mean that we should hold out faith and hope in times of stress, knowing that God will make a way out of no way. If you find yourself in a desperate situation and you've prayed to the God who supplies all your needs according to His riches in glory (see Philippians 4:19), you can activate the angels of provision to help you.

Angelic Activation Prayer

Father, I thank you that you have not called me to lack. You've called me to be in health and prosper even as my soul prospers (see 3 John 1:2). Thank you, Lord, that you've given me the power to create wealth so that I might establish Your covenant in the earth (see Deuteronomy 8:18). I thank You, God, that the righteous will never be forsaken, nor will their children have to beg for bread (see Psalm 37:25). Father, in the name of Jesus, I am asking you to send angels of provision to help me escape this financial bind. Thank you, Lord, for your angels of provision.

16

Activating Angels of Direction

Although the Holy Spirit is our guide—and dwells inside of us—God can choose to send angels to provide direction in our lives. We see this in the life of Abraham's servant. Abraham made his servant swear not to allow his son, Isaac, to take a wife from among the Canaanites. The patriarch charged his servant with going back to his homeland to find a wife for his beloved son. The servant was a little nervous about fulfilling this duty. We read the account in Genesis 24:5–8:

> *Then the servant said to him, "Perhaps the woman will not be willing to follow me to this land. Must I take your son back to the land from which you came?"*
>
> *Abraham said to him, "See to it that you do not take my son back there. The Lord God of heaven, who took me from my father's family and from the land of my relatives, and who spoke to me and swore to me, saying, 'To your descendants I will give this land,' He*

> *shall send His angel before you and you shall take a wife for my son from there. If the woman is not willing to follow you, then you will be free from my oath. Only do not take my son back there."*

Fast-forward a few verses to see Abraham's prophecy to his servant manifest. The servant's steps were ordered directly to the well at which Rebekah was heading to get water for the sheep. The servant's timing was absolutely perfect. Had he come sooner or later, he may have missed Rebekah. How the angel on assignment set the stage for this meeting, we do not know. But we do know that Abraham had prophesied that an angel would go before him—and we see the result of that declaration. It was a divine connection.

God can send angel on assignment to direct you, also. He can choose to activate angels to go before you to make a way for you. Always ask the Lord for direction and wait upon Him to answer you. If you are not discerning His direction—or if you are heading out on the path He shows you—you can activate angels of direction to help guide you along your journey. Remember, though, ultimately the Lord is ordering your steps (see Proverbs 16:9)—He may just be using an angel on assignment to support you.

Angelic Activation Prayer

Father, I thank You for your wisdom and grace in knowing how to help me navigate difficult circumstances. You are wise and all-knowing, and your intentions toward me are kind (see Ephesians 1:5). I petition You now, in Jesus' name, to help me discern Your direction at all times. I ask you, in the name of Your Son, to send angels of direction to help me reach the divine connections and destinations in my life according to Your will. Thank you for directing me in Your paths.

17

Activating Angels of Revelation

God is the primary source of our revelation. Nothing is revealed to us spiritually that is not ultimately revealed by our Father in heaven. As Jesus told Peter when he received the revelation that He was the Christ, the Son of the Living God, flesh and blood does not reveal supernatural concepts to our minds. The Spirit reveals supernatural concepts to our spirit. That said, God can send an angel with a revelation.

We see this principle in Genesis 28, where we read that Jacob left Beersheba and started toward Haran. Setting up camp there, he used a stone as a makeshift pillow and went to sleep. That's when he had a dream. Jacob saw a ladder set up on the earth and reaching into heaven. Let's read the account:

> *The angels of God were ascending and descending on it. The Lord stood above it and said, I am the Lord God of Abraham your father and the God of Isaac. The land on which you lie, to you will I give it and to your descendants. Your descendants will be like the*

dust of the earth, and you will spread abroad to the west and to the east and to the north and to the south, and in you and in your descendants all the families of the earth will be blessed.

"Remember, I am with you, and I will protect you wherever you go, and I will bring you back to this land. For I will not leave you until I have done what I promised you." Jacob awoke out of his sleep, and he said, "Surely the Lord is in this place, and I did not know it." He was afraid and said, "How awesome is this place! This is none other but the house of God, and this is the gate of heaven."

GENESIS 28:11–17

Angelic activity was common in the life of Abraham and even more common in the life of Isaac and Jacob. In Genesis 28, we see angels opening a gateway of revelation to heaven. We see the angel of revelation visiting Jacob again in a dream in Genesis 31:10–13:

When the livestock conceived, I lifted up my eyes and saw in a dream that the male goats mating with the flock were striped, speckled, and spotted. The angel of God spoke to me in a dream, saying, "Jacob." And I said, "Here I am." He said, "Now lift up your eyes and see all the male goats which mate with the flock are striped, speckled, and spotted, for I have seen all that Laban has done to you. I am the God of Bethel, where you anointed the pillar, where you vowed a vow to Me. Now arise, and get out of this land, and return to the land of your family."

Although the Holy Spirit illuminates the plans of God in our lives, our Father in heaven can choose to send angels on assignment—even in our dreams—to offer us revelation necessary for our journey. When you are hard-pressed for revelation in a situation, you can ask the Lord for revelation, pray in the Spirit, ask the Lord for dreams by night and visions by day—and activate the angels of revelation at His leading.

Angelic Activation Prayer

Father, I thank You that You are a God who reveals Your plans and purposes to His people. You are all-knowing, and You reveal your will to us, step by step, as we follow Your heart. I ask You, Lord, in the name of Jesus, to send angels of revelation to assist me in seeing what you see when I can't otherwise see it. Send angels to reveal your strategies and tactics in dreams and visions, according to Your will.

In Jesus' name.

18

Activating Forerunner Angels

John the Baptist was a forerunner for Jesus, preparing the way for the First Coming of our Lord and Savior (see Mark 1:2–3). Jesus Christ is also called a forerunner (see Hebrews 6:20). The Greek word for "forerunner" is *prodromos*, which means "one who is sent before to take observations or act as a spy, a scout, a light armed soldier; one who comes in advance to a place where the rest are to follow."

In the Bible, we also see angels, who are like prophetic servants, functioning as forerunners. We see angels also go before God's people to make a way for them in the natural realm. Exodus 23:20–23 reads:

> *Indeed, I am going to send an angel before you to guard you along the way and to bring you into the place which I have prepared. Be on guard before him and obey his voice. Do not provoke him, for he will not pardon your transgressions, for My name is in him. But if you diligently obey his voice and do all that I say, then I will be an enemy to your enemies and an adversary to your adversaries. For My angel will go before you and bring you to the Amorites,*

and the Hittites, and the Perizzites, and the Canaanites, the Hivites, and the Jebusites, and I will completely destroy them.

We also see forerunner angels in Exodus 33:1–3 as part of the Lord's promise to Moses and the children of Israel as they walked through the wilderness:

Then the Lord said to Moses, "Depart, go up from here, you and the people whom you have brought up from the land of Egypt, to the land which I swore to Abraham, Isaac, and Jacob, saying, 'To your descendants I will give it.' I will send an angel before you, and I will drive out the Canaanite, the Amorite, the Hittite, the Perizzite, the Hivite, and the Jebusite. Go up to a land flowing with milk and honey. However, I will not go up in your midst, for you are a stiff-necked people, and I might destroy you on the way."

God can and does send angels to go first. Jesus is our ultimate forerunner, but the Holy Spirit may lead you to activate forerunner angels, especially when you are pioneering, blazing new trails, and taking new ground.

Angel Activation Prayer

Father, I thank you that Jesus has entered for us as a forerunner, our everlasting High Priest after the order of Melchizedek (see Hebrews 6:20). I thank you, Lord, for sending Jesus to make a way for my salvation. As I enter new territory, I thank You that You go before me and that you are my rear guard (see Isaiah 52:12 and Isaiah 58:8). Father, I ask you in the name of Jesus to release forerunner angels to clear stumbling blocks, hindrances, and other obstacles from my path. I loose forerunner angels, in the name of Jesus, to make the crooked paths straight. Thank you, Jesus, for dispatching forerunner angels as I move into my next assignment for Your glory.

19

Activating Deliverance Angels

Deliverance is mentioned over and over in the Bible. God is our ultimate deliverer (see Psalm 42:11). We see God working deliverance for Moses and the Israelites (see Exodus 5:2), through various judges (see Judges 15:18), to David, through the actions of Queen Esther, and many others. Over and over, the Psalms speak of deliverance.

In both the Hebrew and the Greek languages, deliverance is included in the concept of salvation. In fact, "deliverance" means "salvation." One Hebrew word for deliverance is *yesha*, which means "deliverance, rescue, salvation, safety, welfare," according to *Strong's Concordance*.

The Greek word for salvation is *sozo*, which means:

> ...to save, keep safe and sound, to rescue from danger or destruction; to save a suffering one (from perishing), i.e. one suffering from disease, to make well, heal, restore to health; to preserve one who is in danger of destruction, to save or rescue; to deliver from the penalties of the Messianic judgment; and to save from the evils which obstruct the reception of the Messianic deliverance.

Are you getting the picture? God wants to deliver us from evil, which is why Jesus offered that line as part of the Lord's Prayer (see Matthew 6:9–13). At times, God sends angels on assignment with a deliverance mission. Angels can't save our souls, but they can rescue us from danger.

DRAMATIC ANGELIC DELIVERANCES

Deliverance can be dramatic at times—especially when angels are involved. We read about how God sent angels of deliverance on assignment in Numbers 20:14–16:

> *Moses sent messengers from Kadesh to the king of Edom, "Thus says your brother Israel: You know all the hardship that has found us, how our fathers went down into Egypt, and we lived in Egypt a long time, and the Egyptians distressed us and our fathers. And when we cried out to the Lord, He heard our voice and sent an angel and brought us out of Egypt."*

Daniel experienced the saving power of deliverance angels when he was in the lion's den. As the story goes, Daniel had a habit of praying to Jehovah three time a day. Seeking to snare him, Daniel's enemies talked King Darius into establishing a royal statute and decree that no one could pray to any God or man for thirty days. Daniel understood the decree, but refused to compromise his faith in God. Daniel continued praying, and Darius was forced to enforce his decree. Daniel 6:17–22 tells us about the angelic intervention:

> *A stone was brought and laid upon the mouth of the den, and the king sealed it with his own signet and with the signet of his lords so that nothing might be changed concerning Daniel. Then the king*

went to his palace and passed the night fasting, and no instruments of music were brought before him. And his sleep fled from him.

Then the king arose very early in the morning and went in haste to the den of lions. When he came to the den, he cried with a voice full of sorrow to Daniel. And the king spoke and said to Daniel, "Daniel, servant of the living God, has your God whom you serve continually been able to deliver you from the lions?"

Then Daniel said to the king, "O king, live forever! My God has sent His angel and has shut the lions' mouths so that they have not hurt me, because innocence was found in me before Him; and also before you, O king, I have done no harm."

When Angels Deliver Apostles

In the New Testament, we find the apostles in sticky situations time and time again. James, the brother of Jesus, was martyred for the sake of the gospel, but other apostles were delivered. Angels of deliverance on assignment rescued apostles in Acts 5:17–20:

Then the high priest and all those who were with him (that is, the sect of the Sadducees) rose up and were filled with jealousy. They seized the apostles and put them in the common prison. But during the night an angel of the Lord opened the prison doors and led them out, and said, "Go, stand and speak in the temple to the people all the words of this life."

God sent an angel of deliverance on a stealth assignment, below the radar screen of the guards. The angel not only brought freedom, but instruction. We see that angels, then, can serve more than one function or purpose while on assignment.

Peter was in dire straits when an angel of deliverance encountered him. Naturally speaking, there was absolutely no way he could break free from the predicament in which he found himself. He was in the equivalent of a maximum-security prison when the angels found him facing sure death at the hand of Herod. Thankfully, God sent the angels of deliverance to set Peter free. We read about this amazing account in Acts 12:6–11:

> *The very night when Herod would have brought him out, Peter was sleeping between two soldiers, bound with two chains. And the guards before the door were securing the prison. And suddenly an angel of the Lord approached him, and a light shone in the prison. He struck Peter on the side and woke him up, saying, "Rise up, quickly." And the chains fell off his hands.*
>
> *Then the angel said to him, "Dress yourself and put your sandals on." And he did so. Then he said to him, "Wrap your cloak around you and follow me." He went out and followed him, and did not know that what was done by the angel was real, but thought he was seeing a vision.*
>
> *When they had passed the first and the second guards, they came to the iron gate leading to the city, which opened to them by itself. And they went out and went forward one street. And immediately the angel left him. When Peter had come to himself, he said, "Now I certainly know that the Lord has sent His angel and delivered me from the hand of Herod and from all that the Jewish people were expecting."*

Peter said it right out of his own mouth: *An angel delivered him.* We know Jesus is our Deliverer. In the name of Jesus, the power of God unto deliverance is released. We put our hope and trust in God for deliverance from demons and dangerous situations. Like the psalmist said: "My soul longs for Your deliverance, but I hope in Your word." And again, "I will thank You that You have heard me and have become my deliverance" (Psalm 119:123). Yet again, "Lord, I have hoped for Your deliverance, and I carry out Your commandments" (Psalm 119:166).

That said, God can and does send angels of deliverance on assignment as we see in Scripture repeatedly. Man may seize us, but God can choose to deliver us by the hand of angels. We have no evidence that the apostles—or Daniel—prayed for deliverance angels. But we have no evidence that they didn't, either. If you find yourself in a perilous situation, the Holy Spirit may lead you to activate the angels of deliverance.

Angelic Activation Prayer

Father, I thank You that You have assigned angels of deliverance to serve in Your kingdom. Although I recognize you as my rock, my fortress, and my deliverer (see Psalm 18:2)—and a very present help in my time of need (see Psalm 46:1), I also recognize the reality of deliverance angels. In the name of Jesus, I ask You to send these ministering spirits to minister deliverance to me in my current situation. I take authority over the wicked powers of the enemy, binding the hand of the oppressor, and loose angels of deliverance, in the name of Jesus. Thank You, Lord, for Your delivering power to rescue me.

20

Activating Angels of Interpretation

We see over and over in Scripture—in both the Old and New Testaments—the Lord sending angels on assignment to help prophets interpret dreams and visions. Zechariah needed some help, and finds it, as we see recorded in Zechariah 1:8–10:

> *I saw during the night a man riding on a red horse. But he was standing among the myrtle trees that were in the ravine, and behind him were red, sorrel, and white horses. And I said, "What are these, my lord?" Then the angel who was speaking with me said, "I will show you what these are." Then the man who was standing among the myrtle trees responded and said, "These are the ones whom the Lord has sent out to walk to and fro on the earth."*

Although Daniel had the gift of interpreting dreams, we see angels of interpretation helping him understand dramatic prophetic events the

Lord shared with the prophet. In Daniel 8, the angel Gabriel helped the prophet make sense of his vision of the ram and goat fighting. Daniel's account of the encounter is in Daniel 8:15–22:

> *When I, Daniel, had seen the vision, I sought for the meaning. Then there before me stood one who had the appearance of a man. I heard a man's voice between the banks of Ulai, which called, and said, "Gabriel, make this man understand the vision. So he came near where I stood. And when he came, I was afraid and fell upon my face; but he said to me, 'Understand, son of man, that the vision deals with the time of the end.'*
>
> *"Now as he was speaking with me, I was in a deep sleep with my face toward the ground. But he touched me and set me upright. He said, 'Listen, I will make you know what shall be in the final period of the indignation, for the end shall be at the appointed time.*
>
> *"'The ram which you saw having two horns represents the kings of Media and Persia. The rough goat is the king of Greece, and the great horn that is between his eyes is the first king. Now the broken horn and the four horns that stood up in its place are four kingdoms that shall stand up out of his nation, but not with his power.'"*

Ask God for the Interpretation

When we have dreams and visions or other supernatural experiences that require interpretation, our first move should be to pray and study the Word of God. The God who gave us the download, encountered our hearts, showed us the vision, or gave us the dream is the One who is best able to offer an accurate interpretation.

While nothing is wrong with presenting our dreams and visions to someone who has skill in interpreting this type of prophetic communication, ultimately, the interpretation belongs to the Lord (see Genesis 41:16). Of course, He can send an angel to unpack a revelation for us. He can—and does—send angels on assignment to interpret supernatural communication. We should seek the Lord for answers, but be open to angels of interpretation to assist us in understanding the will of the Lord.

Remember, though, that true angels of God will not violate Scripture. True angels of God will not speak words that conflict with what we read in the Bible. Angels of light have come to people with interpretations of revelations that caused them to form wrong doctrine and eventually establish false religions and deadly cults.

Paul wrote something worth pondering in his epistle to the Galatians:

> *I marvel that you are turning away so soon from Him who called you in the grace of Christ to a different gospel, which is not a gospel. But there are some who trouble you and would pervert the gospel of Christ. Although if we or an angel from heaven preach any other gospel to you than the one we have preached to you, let him be accursed. As we said before, so I say now again: If anyone preaches any other gospel to you than the one you have received, let him be accursed.*
>
> Galatians 1:6–9

There is only one true gospel—the gospel of Jesus Christ. We're saved by grace through faith, not by works, so we can't boast (see Ephesians 2:9).

I believe we should seek the Holy Spirit's wisdom and study the Word when we receive dreams and visions. The Bible—not dream dictionaries and Internet charts—is the best interpreter of dreams. That said, God can send angels on assignment to share with us the interpretation of dreams and visions, just as he did with Zechariah and Daniel.

Angelic Activation Prayer

Father, I am so grateful that you give me revelation, dreams, and visions. Thank You for sharing with me prophetically what is on your heart for my life and the lives of others. Please give me the interpretation. Help me understand what You are saying. Illuminate Your Word to me. Help me see things the way You do. Give me Your perspective. I activate the angels of interpretation to help me understand what You are saying to me, just as You helped the prophets of old understand what You were showing them.

In Jesus' name.

21

Activating Angels of Rebuke

Angels of rebuke are a reality in the kingdom. "Rebuke" means to correct or scold because we disapprove of an action. When the Lord rebukes, He is actually motivated by love. Hebrews 12:5–8 (AMPC) explains this in depth:

> *My son, do not think lightly or scorn to submit to the correction and discipline of the Lord, nor lose courage and give up and faint when you are reproved or corrected by Him; For the Lord corrects and disciplines everyone whom He loves, and He punishes, even scourges, every son whom He accepts and welcomes to His heart and cherishes.*
>
> *You must submit to and endure [correction] for discipline; God is dealing with you as with sons. For what son is there whom his father does not [thus] train and correct and discipline? Now if you are exempt from correction and left without discipline in which all [of God's children] share, then you are illegitimate offspring and not true sons [at all].*

Hebrews 12:11 goes on to say that nobody really enjoys a rebuke. In fact, it's painful. But if we endure the rebuke, it produces "the peaceable fruit of righteousness." The Amplified Bible calls it "a harvest of fruit which consists in righteousness—in conformity to God's will in purpose, thought, and action, resulting in right living and right standing with God."

We know that the Holy Spirit Himself inspired Scripture, and the Word of God is not only sharper than any two-edged sword and judges the thoughts and intents of the heart (Hebrews 4:12), but it's also profitable in four specific ways: for teaching, reproof, correction, and instruction in righteousness (see 2 Timothy 3:16–17). The Holy Spirit, the same One who inspired Scripture, is the one who convicts of sin (see John 16:8).

With all that said, the Lord can send angels with a rebuke in their mouth. Consider the story of Balaam, the stubborn prophet greedy for gain. In Numbers 22, we read about a king named Balak wanted to hire Balaam to curse Israel because he feared their fierce army. Balak had seen what Israel had done to the Amorites and was concerned his kingdom, Moab, was next. As the story goes, Balak sent messengers to Balaam with the request. The elders of Moab and Midian presented Balaam with a bribe—what the Bible calls "divination payments"—on Balak's behalf.

Balaam's response: "Let me ask God about it." But God came to him first, asking about the man. When Balak reported to Jehovah what happened, God immediately told him, "You will not go with them. You will not curse the people because they are blessed" (Numbers 22:12).

The next morning, Balaam told Balak's representatives that the Lord refused to let him take on the assignment. The servants went on their way, only to return with the promise of both riches and honor if Balaam would curse Israel. Balaam seemed to be standing strong against the temptation, answering:

> *If Balak gave me his house full of silver and gold, I am not able to go beyond the command of the Lord my God, to do less or more.*
>
> NUMBERS 22:18

Nevertheless, Balaam inquired of the Lord, and he thought he got a clearance when the Lord said:

> *If the men come to call you, rise up and go with them. But surely the word which I will say to you, that will you do.*
>
> NUMBERS 22:20

Balaam set out to go with the Moabites, and the Bible says God was angry.

Balaam failed the test. He gave into the temptation to pervert his prophetic gift. He decided one morning to disobey what he knew was the Lord's will. The Bible says he got up in the morning, put a saddle on his donkey, and set out on a journey with the enemies of Israel—the princes of Moab. Numbers 22:22–35 tells the rest of the story:

> *The anger of God was inflamed because he went, and the angel of the Lord stood in the way as an adversary against him. Now he was riding on his donkey, and his two servants were with him. The donkey saw the angel of the Lord standing in the way, and His sword was drawn in His hand, so the donkey turned out of the way and went into the field. Balaam struck the donkey to turn her onto the road.*
>
> *But the angel of the Lord stood in a narrow path of the vineyards, a wall on this side and a wall on that side. When the donkey saw the angel of the Lord, she threw herself into the wall and crushed the foot of Balaam against the wall, and he struck her again.*

The angel of the Lord went further and stood in a narrow place where there was no way to turn either to the right hand or to the left. When the donkey saw the angel of the Lord, she fell down under Balaam, and the anger of Balaam was inflamed, and he struck the donkey with a staff. Then the Lord opened the mouth of the donkey, and she said to Balaam, "What have I done to you, that you have struck me these three times?"

And Balaam said to the donkey, "You have mocked me. O that there was a sword in my hand, for now I would kill you."

The donkey said to Balaam, "Am I not your donkey, whom you have ridden since I became yours, to this day? Do I normally do this to you?"

And he said, "No."

Then the Lord opened the eyes of Balaam, and he saw the angel of the Lord standing in the way, and His sword was drawn in His hand, and he bowed his head and fell flat on his face.

The angel of the Lord said to him, "Why have you struck your donkey these three times? I have come out to oppose you, because your way is perverse before Me. And the donkey saw Me and turned from Me these three times. If she had not turned from Me, surely by now I would have slain you and saved her alive."

Balaam said to the angel of the Lord, "I have sinned because I did not know that You stood in the way against me. Now therefore, if it displeases You, I will return."

The angel of the Lord said to Balaam, "Go with the men. But only speak the word that I tell you to speak." So Balaam went with the leaders of Balak.

It's noteworthy that a donkey had a greater fear of the Lord than a prophet. That may be why the Lord chose to send an angel to rebuke him. It seems that Balaam needed a supernatural encounter to set him on the right path. At the same time, the Lord was intervening for the children of Israel.

Now, if that was the only time the Lord sent an angel on assignment to rebuke someone who was defying His will, it would be evidence enough that angels can function in this capacity. But the Bible gives another witness in Judges 2:1–5:

> *The angel of the Lord went up from Gilgal to Bokim and said, "I brought you up from Egypt and brought you into the land that I promised your fathers." I said, "I will never break My covenant with you, but you must not make a pact with the inhabitants of this land, and you must tear down their altars." Yet you have not obeyed Me. What is this you have done? So now I say, "I will not drive them out before you. They will be thorns in your sides, and their gods will be a snare to you."*
>
> *When the angel of the Lord spoke these words to all the children of Israel, the people raised their voices and wept aloud. They named that place Bokim and sacrificed to the Lord there.*

In both cases of the angel of delivering a message on the Lord's behalf, we see the encounter brought people to repentance. That's the purpose of a rebuke. The Lord is not willing that any should perish, but wants all to come to the knowledge of the truth (see 1 Timothy 2:4).

While we would not activate the angels of rebuke on our behalf—we have the Holy Spirit, the Convincer, living inside of us—the Lord may lead us to activate angels of rebuke, sending them on assignment after lost friend and loved ones. He may lead us to send the angels of rebuke after our prodigals.

Speaking of the Holy Spirit, Jesus said:

And when He comes, He will convict and convince the world and bring demonstration to it about sin and about righteousness (uprightness of heart and right standing with God) and about judgment. About sin, because they do not believe in Me [trust in, rely on, and adhere to Me]; About righteousness (uprightness of heart and right standing with God), because I go to My Father, and you will see Me no longer; About judgment, because the ruler (evil genius, prince) of this world [Satan] is judged and condemned and sentence already is passed upon him.

1 JOHN 16:8–11, AMPC

Angelic Activation Prayer

Father, I thank You that You so loved the world that you sent Your only Son to die on a cross, paying the penalty for sin, which is death (see John 3:16). You didn't send Your Son into the world to condemn the world but to save it. Father, in the name of Jesus, I activate the angels of rebuke to encounter My lost loved ones with your truth. Holy Spirit, bring conviction of sin to our lost loved ones and prodigals and help them see the truth, in Jesus' name. Break the blinders off their eyes. I cast down these arguments that are defying Your Word and Your love, in the name of Your strong Son, Jesus Christ.

22

Activating Angels of Destruction

Activating angels of destruction should not be taken lightly. In other words, this is not an activity we should want to play around with. The Lord does send angels on assignment for destruction, but this function is typically reserved in the canon of Scripture for the Old Testament and the book of Revelation.

We find examples of the angels of destruction in David's time. David decided to take a census of the people, and the Lord's anger burned against Israel as a result. Joab warned David not to conduct the count, but King David overruled him. Joab executed the count. There were eight hundred valiant men in Israel and five hundred thousand in Judah. What happens next is recorded in 2 Samuel 24:10–17:

> *But David's heart smote him after he had numbered the people. David said to the Lord, "I have sinned greatly in what I have*

done. I beseech You, O Lord, take away the iniquity of Your servant, for I have done very foolishly." When David arose in the morning, the word of the Lord came to the prophet Gad, David's seer, saying,

"Go and say to David, 'Thus says the Lord, I hold over you three choices; select one of them, so I may bring it upon you.'" So Gad came to David and told him and said, "Shall seven years of famine come to your land? Or will you flee three months before your pursuing enemies? Or do you prefer three days of pestilence in your land? Consider and see what answer I shall return to Him Who sent me."

And David said to Gad, "I am in great distress. Let us fall into the hands of the Lord, for His mercies are many and great; but let me not fall into the hands of man."

So the Lord sent a plague upon Israel from the morning until the appointed time. Seventy thousand men from the people died, from Dan to Beersheba. When the angel stretched out his hand toward Jerusalem to destroy it, the Lord relented from the calamity. He said to the angel who was annihilating the people, "Enough! Now stay your hand." The angel of the Lord was at the threshing floor of Araunah the Jebusite.

On seeing the angel who was striking down the people, David said to the Lord, "I am the one who has sinned and I am the one who has done wrong. These sheep, what have they done? Please, let your hand be against me and against the house of my father."

Again: Activating angels of destruction should not be taken lightly. This is nothing to engage in when we are angry with an enemy—even demons. Still, there is coming a time when the church will understand the signs of the times and pray in agreement with the Lord's will to call on the angels that will usher destruction into the earth.

PRAYING IN GOD'S JUDGMENTS

Mike Bickle, director of IHOPKC, explains it this way:

> The Church will absolutely be on the earth during the Great Tribulation. Jesus' Bride will partner with Him in this very important time of history at the very climax of this age. The Church will participate in the release of God's judgments under Jesus' leadership through the unified global prayers of faith (Ps. 149:6–9; Mt. 18:18–19; Jn. 14:12; Rev. 8:4; 22:17). The end times is the Church's finest hour, when miracles will occur and supernatural prophetic direction will be released. The miracles of Acts and Exodus will be multiplied and combined on a global level (Mic. 7:15).

Given that this is a controversial view among some in the Body of Christ, let's explore these Scriptures and you can decide for yourself if this view is biblical.

Psalm 149:6–9:

> *Let the high praises of God be in their mouths, and two-edged swords in their hands, to execute vengeance on the nations, and punishments on the peoples; to bind their kings with chains, and their nobles with shackles of iron; to execute upon them the written judgment; this is honor for all His godly ones. Praise the Lord!*[108]

Matthew 18:18–19:

> *Truly I say to you, whatever you bind on earth will be bound in heaven, and whatever you loose on earth will be loosed in heaven. Again I say to you, that if two of you agree on earth about anything they ask, it will be done for them by My Father who is in heaven.*

John 14:12:

Truly, truly I say to you, he who believes in Me will do the works that I do also. And he will do greater works than these, because I am going to My Father.

Revelation 8:4:

The smoke of the incense, with the prayers of the saints, ascended before God from the angel's hand.

Revelation 22:17:

The Spirit and the bride say, "Come." Let him who hears say, "Come." Let him who is thirsty come. Let him who desires take the water of life freely.

Essentially, when the praying church discerns the trumpets, she will pray in the next trumpet to follow. The Bride of Christ will enact on earth what God has ordained in heaven. The church will operate in greater works. It will ultimately release the angels through intercession. At the right time, the Holy Spirit will lead believers into these activation prayers.

23

Activating Reassuring Angels

Angels bring reassurance in times of stress, confusion, or fear. To reassure essentially means to restore one's confidence. It means to console, comfort, solace, soothe, condole, lift up, relieve, or calm. The Holy Spirit is our Comforter, but God can send angels on assignment to reassure us as He wills.

We see one example in Luke 2 as part of the story of Jesus' birth. Some shepherds were in the fields guarding their flocks of sheep when an angel of the Lord suddenly appeared to them. Luke 2:9 describes the Lord's glory surrounding them. Of course, the shepherds were terrified by this encounter—but the angel reassured them with a message:

> *"Don't be afraid!" he said. "I bring you good news that will bring great joy to all people. The Savior—yes, the Messiah, the Lord—has been born today in Bethlehem, the city of David! And you will recognize him by this sign: You will find a baby wrapped snugly in strips of cloth, lying in a manger."*
>
> Luke 2:9–12

That's perhaps the greatest reassurance one could receive, other than Mary at Jesus' tomb, who was also met by an angel with a reassuring message.

> *"Don't be afraid!" he said. "I know you are looking for Jesus, who was crucified. He isn't here! He is risen from the dead, just as he said would happen. Come, see where his body was lying."*
>
> MATTHEW 28:5–6

Again, we should always turn to the Holy Spirit, our Comforter, for reassurance. He dwells inside of us. He is a very present help in time of need (see Psalm 46:1). But the Lord can choose to send angels to reassure us as He has done historically in Scripture. If you are in times of distress—especially over the promises of God—you can pray this prayer.

Angelic Activation Prayer

Father, I thank You that all of your promises are yes and amen (see 2 Corinthians 1:20). You are not a man that you should lie, nor the son of man that you should repent (see Numbers 23:19). I thank You for your faithfulness. Father, in the name of Jesus, please comfort and reassure me by Your Holy Spirit. Send angels according to your will with messages that reassure my heart. I believe; help my unbelief (see Mark 9:24). Reassure me in your great mercy.

24

Activating Angels of Fire

Angels can minister the fire of God to prepare and empower believers for the work of the ministry. Psalm 104:4 tells us that God "makes His ministers a flaming fire." The word "fire" in this verse comes from the Hebrew *'esh*. According to the *KJV Old Testament Hebrew Lexicon*, the word essentially means "fire," but it goes deeper than that. It means "fire, flames, supernatural fire (accompanying theophany), fire (for cooking, roasting, parching), altar-fire or God's anger." In this context, it's a supernatural fire.

Who, then, are His ministers? Psalm 104 is speaking of God's angels. The writer of Hebrews picks up on the psalmist's words, repeating, "Of the angels He says: 'He makes His angels spirits and His servants a flame of fire'" (Hebrews 1:7).

As part of the coming of the Holy Spirit on the day of Pentecost, 120 disciples were all in one place—the Upper Room. The Bible tells us they were praying in unity. Suddenly, a sound like a mighty rushing wind came down from heaven and filled the entire house.

There appeared to them tongues as of fire, being distributed and resting on each of them, and they were all filled with the Holy Spirit and began to speak in other tongues, as the Spirit enabled them to speak.

ACTS 2:3–4

The Greek word for "fire" in Acts 2 is *pur,* which literally means "fire," according to the *KJV New Testament Greek Lexicon.* I believe angels were administering that fire of the Holy Ghost—that baptism of fire. John spoke of a baptism of fire in Matthew 3:11.

What does fire symbolize in the Bible? It can point to the presence of God, as Exodus 3:2–6 shows God speaking to Moses in the burning bush. Paul speaks of Jesus returning "in blazing fire" (see 2 Thessalonians 1:7). John the apostle had clear visions of Jesus with eyes like blazing fire in the context of judgment (see Revelation 1:14; Revelation 2:18; Revelation 19:12). Fire, at times, is also used in relation to the manifestation of God's glory, which appeared like a consuming fire (see Leviticus 9:23–24; Exodus 24:7; and Deuteronomy 5:24).

God's fire consumes sacrifices (see Judges 13:15–10; Judges 6:19–24). God's wrath can burn like fire (see Psalm 89:46). But fire can also purify, as in a refiner's fire (see Malachi 3:3). We see this refining fire in Isaiah's life, administered by an angel. This angel visited the prophet with fire as part of his commissioning. Imagine the scene as described in Isaiah 6:1–7:

In the year that King Uzziah died I saw the Lord sitting on a throne, high and lifted up, and His train filled the temple. Above it stood the seraphim. Each one had six wings. With two he covered his face, and with two he covered his feet, and with two he flew. One cried to another and said: "Holy, holy, holy, is the Lord of Hosts; the whole earth is full of His glory."

The posts of the door moved at the voice of him who cried, and the house was filled with smoke. And I said: "Woe is me! For I am undone because I am a man of unclean lips, and I dwell in the midst of a people of unclean lips. For my eyes have seen the King, the Lord of Hosts."

Then one of the seraphim flew to me with a live coal which he had taken with the tongs from off the altar in his hand. And he laid it on my mouth, and said, "This has touched your lips, and your iniquity is taken away, and your sin purged."

At times, we may need to activate angels of fire in our lives. We may need a fresh baptism of fire. Although the blood of Jesus cleanses us from all unrighteousness, calling for the fire of God to purify us is biblical. At times, the Lord may send angels of fire on His own right. We should embrace the fire of God when it comes, welcoming its purifying aspects in our lives.

Angelic Activation Prayer

Father, I thank You for your fire in my life—the fire that burns away impurities in my heart. Father, baptize me with the Holy Ghost and fire, in the name of Jesus. Set me on fire for You. Make me to burn and shine like John the Baptist (see John 5:35). Help me to keep my lamp filled with oil so I can burn for you in the dark days ahead, in the name of Jesus. Send Your ministers of flaming fire—Your angels—on assignment in my life with Your fire.

25

Activating Angels of Assignment

While there are angels on assignment, sometimes an angel is sent to give the Lord's people an assignment. I believe the Holy Spirit, under the leadership of Jesus, gives us our marching orders in most cases. We know that a prophetic word was released to Barnabas and Saul with an assignment.

> *In the church that was in Antioch there were prophets and teachers: Barnabas, Simeon who was called Niger, Lucius of Cyrene, Manaen who had been brought up with Herod the tetrarch, and Saul. As they worshipped the Lord and fasted, the Holy Spirit said, "Set apart for Me Barnabas and Saul for the work to which I have called them." Then after fasting and praying, they laid their hands on them and sent them off.*
>
> Acts 13:1–3

The Lord can, however, choose to send angels to share our next assignment with us. We find one such angel in 2 Kings 1:3–4:

But the angel of the Lord said to Elijah the Tishbite, "Arise, go up to meet the messengers of the king of Samaria, and say to them, 'Is it because there is not a God in Israel, that you go to inquire of Baal-Zebub the god of Ekron?' Therefore thus says the Lord, 'You will not come down from the bed on which you have gone up but will surely die.'" Then Elijah departed.

We know that the Lord spoke with Elijah on many occasions. This time, though, He chose to send an angel to give him an assignment to meet with a king's messengers. This was not a still, small voice; wind; fire; or an earthquake. It was an angel on assignment with instructions for Elijah.

We also know that Philip was fully of the Holy Ghost and wisdom. He was among the leaders in the early church who was selected based on criteria the apostles set forth. Philip was among the seven "known to be full of the Holy Spirit and wisdom" who were appointed to serve in the early church so the apostles could devote themselves to studying the Word (see Acts 6:3).

Yet we also know that the Lord chose at least once to send an angel to deliver an assignment for Philip. The account is recorded in Acts 8:26–31, and it includes both an angel and the Holy Spirit.

Now an angel of the Lord said to Philip, "Rise up and go toward the south on the way that goes down from Jerusalem to Gaza."

So he rose up and went. And there was a man of Ethiopia, a eunuch of great authority under Candace, queen of the Ethiopians, who was in command of her entire treasury. He had come to Jerusalem to worship. He was returning, sitting in his chariot and reading the book of Isaiah the prophet. The Spirit said to Philip, "Go to this chariot and stay with it."

Then Philip ran to him, and heard him read the book of

Isaiah the prophet, and said, "Do you understand what you are reading?"

He said, "How can I, unless someone guides me?" So he invited Philip to come up and sit with him.

From there, Philip preached the gospel to the eunuch and baptized him in water. Right after that, the evangelist was translated in the spirit to his next assignment (see Acts 8:32–40).

We may choose to activate angels of assignment when we feel stuck. We may discern the Lord preparing us for something new, but also discern enemy resistance. By contrast, we may not understand our purpose, calling, or assignment in any given season. We should always pray to the Father in Jesus' name for the Holy Spirit to separate us unto the work He has called us to do. But there are times He may choose to send angels of assignment to reveal our next exploit.

Angel Activation Prayer

Father, I thank You that You have called me to do even greater works than Jesus (see John 14:2). I am ready and willing, and by Your Spirit I can do all things You've called me to do. I can do all things through Christ who gives me strength (see Philippians 4:13). Please reveal to me my purpose in this season, the next step of my destiny in this hour, by Your Holy Spirit. Lead me forth by peace. Send angels on assignment to show me what I am to do next.

In Jesus' name.

26

Activating Angels of War

Also called warning angels, God sends angels on an assignment to fight for His people in times of war. In the Old Testament, we see examples of this in the physical realm. In the New Testament—in the book of Revelation—we see a war in the heavens. Consider this startling account in 2 Kings 19:34–35:

> *"For I will protect this city to save it, for My own sake and for the sake of David My servant." On that night the angel of the Lord went out and struck one hundred and eighty-five thousand in the camp of the Assyrians. When others woke up early in the morning, these were all dead bodies.*

This reminds me somewhat of how God sent angels to intervene on Israel's behalf in the Six Day War in 1967. Also called the June War or the Third Arab-Israeli War, the Six Day War saw Israel capture the West Bank, Gaza Strip, the Golan Heights, the Sinai Peninsula, and the Old

City of Jerusalem. Israel won this war against all natural odds—Israel's army was outnumbered by about two to one—with the help of a supernatural God and His holy angels on assignment. Stories emerged that the opposition saw angels—and even Abraham—and retreated.

In more recent times, claims of divine intervention were reported in the conflict between Israel and Hamas. WND reported about an operator of Israel's Iron Dome missile defense system, saying he had witnessed "the hand of God" diverting an incoming rocket. Israel Today translated the account from a Hebrew-language news site:

> A missile was fired from Gaza. Iron Dome precisely calculated [its trajectory]. We know where these missiles are going to land down to a radius of 200 meters. This particular missile was going to hit either the Azrieli Towers, the Kirya (Israel's equivalent of the Pentagon) or [a central Tel Aviv railway station]. Hundreds could have died.
>
> We fired the first [interceptor]. It missed. Second [interceptor]. It missed. This is very rare. I was in shock. At this point we had just four seconds until the missile lands. We had already notified emergency services to converge on the target location and had warned of a mass-casualty incident.
>
> Suddenly, Iron Dome (which calculates wind speeds, among other things) shows a major wind coming from the east, a strong wind that...sends the missile into the sea. We were all stunned. I stood up and shouted, "There is a God!"
>
> "I witnessed this miracle with my own eyes. It was not told or reported to me. I saw the hand of God send that missile into the sea."[109]

Was this the hand of God or the work of angels? We don't know for sure, but it's likely that it was angels who had been sent on assignment.

David Asked God for Angels of War

As mighty as David was in battle—after all, he defeated Goliath with a sling and a stone when the rest of the children of Israel were shaking in their boots, and he sang songs about how he slew tens of thousands (see 1 Samuel 18:7)—he still called on angels of war in times of distress. David prayed to the Lord to send angels on assignment to fight for him in war in Psalm 34. Notice how David depends on the Lord, but still calls for the angels.

> Plead my cause, O Lord, with my adversaries; fight those who fight me. Take hold of the large shield and small shield, and rise up for my help. Draw the spear and javelin against those who pursue me. Say to my soul, "I am Your salvation."
>
> May those who seek my life be ashamed and humiliated; may those who plan my injury be turned back and put to shame. May they be as chaff before the wind, and may the angel of the Lord cast them down. May their way be dark and slippery, and may the angel of the Lord pursue them. For without cause they have hidden their net for me in a pit, which they have dug without cause for my soul.

Jesus Himself mentioned angels in the context of war on the night of His betrayal in the Garden of Gethsemane. Peter's first response to the soldiers trying to take Jesus into custody was to pull out his sword and fight. But Jesus corrected him in Matthew 26:52–54:

> *Then Jesus said to him, "Put your sword back in its place. For all those who take up the sword will perish by the sword. Do you think that I cannot now pray to My Father, and He will at once give Me more than twelve legions of angels? But how then would the Scriptures be fulfilled, that it must be so?"*

In the book of Revelation, we read about an epic war between good and evil—a battle between the archangel Michael and his angels and a cohort of demons. The dramatic account is recorded in Revelation 12:6–8, demonstrating the warring nature of some angels on assignment.

> *The woman fled into the wilderness where she has a place prepared by God, that they may nourish her there for one thousand two hundred and sixty days. Then war broke out in heaven. Michael and his angels fought against the dragon, and the dragon and his angels fought, but they did not prevail, nor was there a place for them in heaven any longer.*

The weapons of our warfare are not carnal, but mighty in God for pulling down strongholds (see 2 Corinthians 10:4). Angels are not weapons, but they are on God's side and God is for us. If God is for us, who can be against us? (see Romans 8:31). God has given us authority to bind and loose in the name of Jesus (see Matthew 16:19), but there are times when He will send angels to help us in battle. We'll take a closer look at angel armies later in the book. But for now, understand that when we wage warfare, heaven is on our side. You can pray this activation prayer when you feel you need supernatural backup.

Angel Activation Prayer

Father, I thank You that if You are for me, who can be against me? (see Romans 8:31). I thank You that You are a warrior! You have made me a warrior! You always lead me into triumph in Christ Jesus (see 2 Corinthians 2:14). Thank You for victory in every battle. Thank You for wisdom, strategies, and insight from the Holy Spirit. Thank You for my supernatural weapons. And thank You for Your warring angels. I ask You to dispatch them now, on my behalf.

In Jesus' name.

27

Activating Angels to Prophets

Throughout the Old Testament, we see angels interacting with prophets. God sends angels on assignment to deliver specific messages to prophets. We see one example in 1 Chronicles 21:18. An angel of the Lord commanded Gad to tell David he should go build an altar to the Lord on Ornan's threshing floor. David listened to Gad, who listened to the angel. Apparently, the angel went along to see that the command was carried out. In 1 Chronicles 21:19–30, we read:

> *Now Ornan turned and saw the angel, but his four sons who were with him hid themselves as Ornan threshed the wheat. As David came to Ornan, Ornan looked and saw David and went out from the threshing floor and bowed down before David with his face to the ground. Then David said to Ornan, "Give me the site of the threshing floor so that I may build an altar on it to the Lord. Sell it to me at full price so the plague on the people may be restrained."*
>
> *So Ornan replied to David, "Take it for yourself, and let my lord the king do whatever seems good in his eyes. Look, I will give*

the oxen for the burnt offerings, the threshing wagons for wood, and the wheat for the grain offering. I will give it all."

Then King David said to Ornan, "No, for I will surely acquire it for the full price, for I will not take what is yours for the Lord nor offer burnt offerings that cost me nothing."

So David gave Ornan six hundred shekels[a] of gold by weight for the site, and David built there an altar to the Lord and offered up burnt offerings and peace offerings. He called on the Lord, and the Lord answered him by fire from heaven on the altar of burnt offering.

So the Lord spoke to the angel, and he put away his sword in its sheath. At that time, when David saw that the Lord had answered him at the threshing floor of Ornan the Jebusite, he sacrificed there. For the tabernacle of the Lord and the altar of burnt offering that Moses had made in the wilderness were in the high place in Gibeon at that time. But David was unable to go before it to inquire of God, because he was terrified by the sword of the angel of the Lord.

If you are a prophet, angelic encounters may already be opening to you. Even if you are not a prophet, the last-days prophecy from Joel that Peter announced in Acts 2:17 sets the stage for you to expect angels to deliver messages to you. Acts 2:17 reads:

"In the last days it shall be," says God "that I will pour out My Spirit on all flesh; your sons and your daughters shall prophesy, your young men shall see visions, and your old men shall dream dreams."

You can pray this activation prayer to open your eyes and ears to angels communicating prophetically.

Angelic Activation Prayer

Father, I am grateful that You have a prophetic mandate on my life according to Acts 2:17. I expect to hear from You. I expect to prophesy. I expect to have dreams. I expect to see visions. I expect to experience angelic encounters according to Your will. Please open my eyes and ears to angelic messengers on assignment.

In Jesus' name.

28

Activating Angels of Guarding

Also called guardian angels, these angels on assignment guard God's people. We read about these angels in one of the most oft-quoted passages in Scripture. Psalm 34:7 reads:

> *The angel of the Lord camps around those who fear Him, and delivers them.*

Psalm 91:9–12, another popular passage that reveals the existence of guardian angels, assures us:

> *Because you have made the Lord, who is my refuge, even the Most High, your dwelling, there shall be no evil befall you, neither shall any plague come near your tent; for He shall give His angels charge over you to guard you in all your ways. They shall bear you up in their hands, lest you strike your foot against a stone.*

Although there's debate over whether every person has a guardian angel, Matthew 18:10 (AMP) suggests that we may have more than one angel assigned to us:

See that you do not despise or think less of one of these little ones, for I say to you that their angels in heaven [are in the presence of and] continually look upon the face of My Father who is in heaven.

Given this and the psalms, it seems reasonable to believe that if we don't have "guardian" angels assigned to us, God will send them on assignment as He chooses. You can pray this prayer to activate guardian angels in your life.

Angelic Activation Prayer

Father, I thank You that You are my rock, my fortress, and my deliverer. You are my protector and provider. I thank You, too, that You send angels to guard Your people. I decree and declare Psalm 34:7 over my life—that Your angels are encamped around me and will deliver me from evil because I fear You. I decree and declare Psalm 91 over my life—that You have given Your angels charge over me to guard me in all my ways. I glorify You, my good, good Father. In Jesus' name.

29

Activating Angels of His Presence

The Lord inhabits the praises of His people (see Psalm 22:3). Just as angels stand in the presence of God, angels stand in our presence—whether we discern them or not.

Isaiah spoke of the angels of His presence:

> *For He said, "Surely they are My people, sons who will not lie." So He became their Savior. In all their affliction He was afflicted, and the angel of His presence saved them; in His love and in His mercy He redeemed them; and He lifted them and carried them all the days of old.*
>
> Isaiah 63:8–10

This seems to imply an angel of comfort or God's own personal presence. I believe the angel of His presence ministers the presence of God. In His presence is fullness of joy (see Psalm 16:11). Where His presence is, we find rest (see Psalm 27:8). Times of refreshing come in the presence of the Lord (see Acts 3:20–21). I believe angels of His presence minister all of these things.

Of course, the Holy Spirit Himself is our comforter, our peace, and our joy. But the Lord can send angels of His presence to minister to us. Pray this prayer if you are in desperate need of angels of His presence to help you receive the ministry of the Holy Spirit.

Angelic Activation Prayer

Father, in the name of Jesus, I thank You that You are my light and my salvation (see Psalm 27:1). Jesus is my Prince of Peace (see Isaiah 9:6). The Holy Spirit is my Comforter. Your joy is my strength (see Nehemiah 8:10). I exalt you, Father. Right now, I am having a difficult time pressing into Your presence with all the mind traffic and distractions. Draw me close to You. Woo me by Your Spirit. Send angels of Your Presence to minister Your Presence to me.

In Jesus' name.

30

Activating Angels of Communication

God sends angelic messengers on assignment to communicate a message. These angels can come in many forms, or they may appear in dreams or visions. After the Holy Spirit came upon Mary in the immaculate conception, Joseph intended to divorce her privately.

> *But while he thought on these things, the angel of the Lord appeared to him in a dream saying, "Joseph, son of David, do not be afraid to take Mary as your wife, for He who is conceived in her is of the Holy Spirit. She will bear a Son, and you shall call His name Jesus, for He will save His people from their sins."*
>
> Matthew 1:20–21

After Jesus died on the cross and was buried in a tomb, Mary Magdalene and another woman named Mary went to the grave site. In this scene, the angel wore garments that were as white as snow, and his countenance was like lightning. That caused the angels who were guarding the tomb to shake in fear and pass out. The angel communicated a message:

> *The angel said to the women, "Do not be afraid. For I know that you are looking for Jesus who was crucified. He is not here. For He has risen, as He said. Come, see the place where the Lord lay."*
>
> MATTHEW 28:5–6

We should seek the Lord for His wisdom, His prophetic words, and His messages. The Lord communicates in various ways to His people. That said, one way He can choose to communicate to us is through the ministry of angels. You can pray this prayer for greater awareness of angelic communication.

Angelic Activation Prayer

Father, in the name of Jesus, I thank You that You speak to my heart. I thank You that I know Your voice, and the voice of another I will not follow (see John 10:27). I thank You, Lord, that you can speak to me in a still, small voice; in dreams and visions; through nature—and through angels. Open my spiritual ears to help me hear You however you may choose to send me messages—even through angels, in Jesus' name.

I give You praise, God.

31

Activating Angels of Strengthening

Angels are sent to minister to the heirs of salvation (see Hebrews 1:14), but they also ministered to the Author of Salvation, our Lord Jesus Christ, in the wilderness. After Jesus was baptized in the Jordan River, the Holy Spirit came upon Him and drove Him into the wilderness where He was temped for forty days. Matthew 4:11: says:

> *Then the devil left Him, and immediately angels came and ministered to Him.*

Paul also encountered angels of strengthening—or rather, angels of strengthening encountered him. We read of his perilous journey in Acts 27:17:

> *When they had hoisted it aboard, they used ropes to undergird the ship. And fearing that they might run aground on the sand of Syrtis, they let down the mast, and so were driven. We were violently tossed by the storm. The next day they threw cargo*

overboard. On the third day we threw the tackle of the ship overboard with our own hands. When neither sun nor stars appeared for many days, and no small storm was upon us, all hope that we should be saved was lost.

After they had long abstained from food, Paul stood in their midst and said, "Men, you should have listened to me and not have set sail from Crete, incurring this injury and loss. But now I advise you to take courage, for there will be no loss of life among you, but only of the ship. For there stood by me this night the angel of God to whom I belong and whom I serve, saying, 'Do not be afraid, Paul. You must stand before Caesar. And, look! God has given you all those who sail with you.' Therefore, men, take courage, for I believe God that it will be exactly as it was told to me."

God is the source of our strength. The spirit that raised Christ from the dead dwells inside of us (see Romans 8:11). Still, God can choose to send angels to strengthen us. You can pray this activation prayer when you feel weak and need all the help you can get from God. After all, Daniel 7:25 makes it clear that Satan, a fallen angel, is setting out to wear you out. It only makes sense that God's angels could help strengthen you.

Angelic Activation Prayer

Father, in the name of Jesus, I thank You that You are my Strengthener. Your strength sustains me. Your grace is sufficient for anything and everything I may encounter (see 2 Corinthians 12:9). Yet I see that You sent angels to strengthen Jesus and Paul, and I am weary in well doing. I don't want to faint and give up my harvest. Strengthen me by Your Spirit and Your Word. Send angels to strengthen me according to Your will.

In Jesus' name.

32

Activating the Angels of Transition

The Lord spoke these words to me:

> Many neglect the angels of transition, and they bypass the help I have sent to transition them into the next stage of their journey. Many ignore the angels of transition and therefore fail to enter into the new place I have set aside for them at the appointed time. Many are working in their own strength, struggling in the flesh and failing to embrace the work of My angels on assignment to help them transition into the new thing. Look for the angels in times of transition.

Some transitions are traumatic, like losing a loved one, getting divorced, or losing a job. Other transitions are exciting, like graduating college, getting married, or moving into a dream home. How well we navigate transition depends on at least six things: (1) how much we trust God, (2) how well we know the Word, (3) how willing we are to yield to the Spirit, (4) how we conduct our prayer and fasting life (5) how intimate we are with God, (6) how much we determine to persevere, (6) who we choose to have around us, and (8) whether we embrace the work of angels to help us. Only God can transition us from glory to glory; angels are there to help us.

Angelic Activation Prayer

Father, in the name of Jesus, I thank You for angels of transition. I ask You to release them into my life to help me break through to the other side. I thank You for the leading and guiding of Your Holy Spirit, and ask You to send ministering spirits right now to help me transition through this difficult time.

In Jesus' name.

33

Activating Reaping Angels

The Lord will send angels on assignment to help reap the final harvest of souls. Angels can also reap in other areas the Lord wills. "Reap" means, essentially, "to gather." Reaping angels, or gathering angels, can bring in a harvest of any kind on God's command. Jesus speaks of the reaping angels in the explanation of the Parable of the Sower in Matthew 13:36–40:

> *Then Jesus sent the crowds away and went into the house. And His disciples came to Him, saying, "Explain to us the parable of the weeds of the field." He answered, "He who sows the good seed is the Son of Man, the field is the world, and the good seed are the sons of the kingdom. But the weeds are the sons of the evil one.*
>
> *"The enemy who sowed them is the devil, the harvest is the end of the world, and the reapers are the angels. Therefore as the weeds are gathered and burned in the fire, so shall it be in the end of this world. The Son of Man shall send out His angels, and they shall gather out of His kingdom all things that offend, and those who do evil, and will throw them into a fiery furnace. There will be wailing and gnashing of teeth."*

In the context of the end-times drama, we again see Jesus talking about gathering angels. Matthew 24:31 reads:

> *And He will send His angels with a great sound of a trumpet, and they shall gather His elect from the four winds, from one end of the heavens to the other.*

I would be remiss if I didn't mention a profound prophecy the Lord gave me about the angels of abundant harvest, which are essentially reaping angels. The Lord spoke these words to me:

> An abundant harvest is at hand. I am releasing angels of abundant harvest into the nation. You will reap what you have sown. This is a double-edged sword.
>
> Where the enemy has resisted your harvest in years past, you will see a multiplication effect of blessing in your life. Doors will open unto you that no man can open. Opportunities will come your way that you never dreamed, imagined, or even thought to ask for. Provision will enter your life from unexpected places.
>
> If you have sown to the spirit, you will reap from the spirit. If you have sown into My kingdom business, you will see a return on the investment of your time, your finances, and your relationships. Reinforcement will come to support the work of your hand. You will find that lack is no longer in your language. You will see blessings chase you down and overtake you. You will find that I am leading you and guiding you with greater precision. You will hear My voice and dream My dreams and see My visions. You will rest in Me and have confidence and faith in me that defies the enemy's plans for your life. This is a year of abundant harvest.
>
> I will not be mocked. Whatever a man sows he will reap. There are laws of the harvest and they are in effect.

If you have been holding back what belongs to Me, release it. If you have been muzzling the ox, loose him. If you have been sowing seeds of discord among My children, go to them in humility and make it right. If you have been defying My will, get in alignment with Me now.

I am releasing the angels of abundant harvest. They will minister blessings to the heirs of salvation. They will bring provision and protection from the enemy's sword. I am releasing the angels of abundant harvest. Make your choice. Choose this day whom you will serve with your whole heart. I am a God of justice. I am also a God of mercy.

You have put me to the test in the last season and a season of abundant harvest is coming into your life. Prepare your hearts now to receive what is in store for you. I am Your God and I love you with an everlasting love. I am releasing angels of abundant harvest.

I wrote a book based on this prophecy and how to abide by the laws of the harvest, how to avoid hindering or offending our angels, and more. (Find this book at angelsprophecy.com).

You can activate angels of abundant harvest in your life using the Word of God. Pray the prayer below, and find more like this in my book, *Releasing the Angels of Abundant Harvest.*

Angelic Activation Prayer

Father, I thank You for the abundant harvest You have stored up for me. I thank You that I will reap what I sow exponentially. I activate the angels of abundant harvest even now to reap what belongs to me, take back what the enemy stole, and bring in what you've called me to have.

In Jesus' name.

34

Activating Angels of Protection

Perhaps different from guardian angels assigned to believers, angels of protection are on assignment to protect us in the face of danger. These angels may not deliver us from the midst of danger, but protect us from harm. An angel protected Shadrach, Meshach, and Abednego in the fiery furnace in Daniel 3.

Consider the back story. King Nebuchadnezzar decreed that everyone who hears the sound of music should fall down and worship a golden image—and whoever refuses to do so would be cast into a fiery furnace. A group of Chaldeans went to the king and told him Shadrach, Meshach, and Abednego were not bowing to the image. The king was furious and commanded the boys to be brought before him to ask if it were true.

> *Shadrach, Meshach, and Abednego answered and said to the king, "O Nebuchadnezzar, we do not need to give you an answer in this matter. If it be so, our God whom we serve is able to deliver us from the burning fiery furnace, and He will deliver us out of*

> *your hand, O king. But even if He does not, be it known to you, O king, that we will not serve your gods, nor worship the golden image which you have set up."*
>
> DANIEL 3:16–18

The king was so angry that he commanded his servants to turn up the heat on the furnace seven times hotter than usual. The boys were bound and cast into the fire. The fire was so hot that it instantly killed the men who bound the boys.

> *Then Nebuchadnezzar the king was astonished, and rose up in haste, and spoke, and said to his counselors, "Did we not cast three men bound into the midst of the fire?"*
>
> *They answered and said to the king, "True, O king."*
>
> *He answered and said, "But I see four men loose and walking in the midst of the fire, and they are unharmed. And the form of the fourth is like the Son of God!"*
>
> *Then Shadrach, Meshach, and Abednego came out of the midst of the fire. The officials, governors, and captains, and the king's counselors, being gathered together, saw these men upon whose bodies the fire had no power, nor was a hair of their head singed, neither were their coats changed, nor had the smell of fire even come upon them.*
>
> *Then Nebuchadnezzar spoke and said, "Blessed be the God of Shadrach, Meshach, and Abednego, who has sent His angel and delivered His servants who trusted in Him. They have defied the king's word, and yielded their bodies, that they might not serve nor worship any god, except their own God."*
>
> DANIEL 3:24–28

An angel spoke to Moses sternly about angelic protection in Exodus 23:20–22:

> *Indeed, I am going to send an angel before you to guard you along the way and to bring you into the place which I have prepared. Be on guard before him and obey his voice. Do not provoke him, for he will not pardon your transgressions, for My name is in him. But if you diligently obey his voice and do all that I say, then I will be an enemy to your enemies and an adversary to your adversaries.*

We can ask the Lord to send angels on assignment to protect us in the midst of danger and turmoil. Of course, we must always remember that our help comes from the Lord. He is our ultimate defender, rescuer, and source of protection.

Angelic Activation Prayer

Father, in the name of Jesus, I thank You for protecting angels to keep me in the midst of dangerous situations. I may never be thrown into a jail, a pit, or a furnace, but I find may find myself in the middle perilous moments where only You can rescue me. I praise You, Lord, my deliverer, and ask you to send protecting angels to keep me if I encounter trouble.

35

Activating Angels of Prophetic Announcement

God releases angels of announcement on assignment at strategic times. He could use prophets, but He chooses to use angels. We see two accounts of this relating to the transition from the old covenant to the new covenant with regard to significant births: John the Baptist and Jesus.

In Luke 1, an angel of the Lord appeared to Zechariah. Of course, he was afraid, but the angel comforted him and assured him he didn't need to fear. Then he announced to the man of God that God had heard his prayer:

> *But the angel said to him, "Do not fear, Zechariah, for your prayer has been heard, and your wife Elizabeth will bear you a son, and you shall call his name John. You will have joy and gladness, and many will rejoice at his birth. For he will be great in the sight of the Lord, and shall drink neither wine nor strong drink, and he will be filled with the Holy Spirit, even from his mother's womb.*

He will turn many of the sons of Israel to the Lord their God. And he will go before Him in the spirit and power of Elijah, to turn the hearts of the fathers to the children and the disobedient to the wisdom of the just, to make ready a people prepared for the Lord."

LUKE 1:13–17

Of course, this was hard for Zechariah to believe. What a prophetic announcement this was! Zechariah asked the angel how this was possible, given that he and his wife Elizabeth were beyond child-bearing years. Gabriel, the messenger, didn't like his response.

The angel answered him, "I am Gabriel, who stands in the presence of God. And I was sent to speak to you and to bring you this good news. And now you will be silent and unable to speak until the day that these things happen, because you did not believe my words, which will be fulfilled in their season."

LUKE 1:19–20

Gabriel, the same angel who later visited Mary with a prophetic announcement (Luke 1) greeted Mary by telling her that she was highly favored, the Lord was with her, and she was blessed among women.

When she saw him, she was troubled by his words, and considered in her mind what kind of greeting this might be. But the angel said to her, "Do not be afraid, Mary, for you have found favor with God. Listen, you will conceive in your womb and bear a Son and shall call His name JESUS. He will be great, and will be called the Son of the Highest. And the Lord God will give Him the throne of His father David, and He will reign over the house of Jacob forever. And of His kingdom there will be no end."

LUKE 1:29–33

Angels make prophetic announcements. This angel didn't just bring news, as in communication or instruction. He angel actually prophesied over these babies. Again, God could have used prophets in these instances, but instead, He used angels. In Revelation 22:9, an angel actually compared himself to "your brothers the prophets." Angels can prophesy what the Lord is saying and doing.

Now, you are your own best prophet. You can hear from God for yourself. You don't need any mediator between you and Jesus. The Holy Spirit lives inside of you. But God can and does send angels to prophesy to people, and we should be open to that.

Angelic Activation Prayer

Father, in the name of Jesus, I thank You that Your ministering spirits sent to minister to the heirs of salvation are prophetic spirits. They hear from You and can deliver prophetic messages about my destiny, just as they did regarding John the Baptist and Jesus. Give me an open heart to receive prophetic messages from Your Spirit, from Your prophets, or from Your angels.

In Jesus' name.

36

Activating Witnessing Angels

God knows everything, yet He chooses to employ witnessing angels. God sends witnessing angels on assignment to accomplish His purposes of chronicling, or recording, human events. We see at least three Bible references to witnessing angels. Let's look at each one in greater detail:

In Luke 12:8–10, Jesus said some sobering words:

> *I say to you, whoever confesses Me before men, him will the Son of Man also confess before the angels of God. But he who denies Me before men will be denied before the angels of God. And everyone who speaks a word against the Son of Man will be forgiven, but he who blasphemes against the Holy Spirit will not be forgiven.*

In the parable of the coins, Jesus again mentions witnessing angels. Luke 15:9–11 reads:

And when she has found it, she calls together her friends and neighbors, saying, "Rejoice with me, for I have found the coin which I had lost. Likewise, I tell you, there is joy in the presence of the angels of God over one sinner who repents."

And in 1 Timothy 5:21, Paul the apostle writes:

I command you before God and the Lord Jesus Christ and the elect angels that you observe these things without prejudice, doing nothing by partiality.

Angels can't see everything and don't know everything. They aren't omnipresent or omniscient. But God can and does send angels on assignment to watch, witness, and record events. You can call on witnessing angels to observe your confessions, your righteous works for the Lord, and your commands as eternal witnesses.

Angelic Activation Prayer

Father, I thank You that all my days are written in Your book. I thank You, God, that You care so much about me that You have a book of remembrance that chronicles the times I esteem your name (Malachi 3:16–18). Send your angels to witness my praise to You that it may be forever recorded, in Jesus' name. Send angels to witness my righteous works, in the name of the Lord.

37

Activating Angels of Instruction

The book of Hebrews opens this way:

> *God, who at various times and in diverse ways spoke long ago to the fathers through the prophets, has in these last days spoken to us by His Son, whom He has appointed heir of all things, and through whom He made the world.*
>
> Hebrews 1:1

God wants to speak with us directly. Communication is part of relationship. But we have seen over and over in Scripture that God, at times, also sends angels on assignment with messages. Some of those angels deliver instructions from on high, from the throne room to our bedrooms. Cornelius, a Gentile, experienced this firsthand.

The Bible describes Cornelius as a centurion and a devout man who walked in the fear of the Lord, though he was a Gentile. The Word tells us that Cornelius gave plenty of alms and prayed to God constantly. One day, an angel of God came to him in a vision, calling his name.

He said to him, "Your prayers and your alms have come up as a memorial before God. Now send men to Joppa, and bring back Simon whose surname is Peter. He is lodging with Simon, a tanner, whose house is by the sea. He will tell you what you must do."

ACTS 10:4–6

Cornelius followed the angel's instructions. He sent for Peter. Peter came by instruction of the Lord through a vision in a trance and asked Cornelius what the matter was. The centurion told the apostle about the angel in the vision, and Peter began preaching the gospel to the Gentile man, who was saved and filled with the Spirit all at once.

God can send angels on assignment with instructions. He can also speak clear instructions to us in a trance, through a prophet, or even through a donkey. The point is, angels of instruction are part of God's communications plan, and you can call for them when all else seems to fail.

Angelic Activation Prayer

Father, I thank You that You are creative in the ways You reach Your people. You reached Peter in a trance. You reached Balaam through a donkey. Lord, I love to hear Your voice, but I am open to receiving instructions from one of Your holy angels on assignment. If I am not catching on to what You are trying to tell me, please send angels of instruction to make it clear.

In Jesus' name.

38

Activating Angels of Prayer Answers

We know that the Lord delights in the prayers of the righteous (see Psalm 15:8). We know that we are the righteousness of God in Christ Jesus (see 2 Corinthians 5:21). We know that if we pray anything according to His will, He hears and answers us (see 1 John 5:14). And we know that the Holy Spirit helps us in our weakness, because many times we don't know what to pray (see Romans 8:26).

What we may not keep in mind is the role of angels of prayer answers. Put another way, God sends angels on assignment to deliver answers to our prayers. This may happen when the bowls in heaven fill up and tip over. We read about these bowls and the role of heavenly beings stewarding them in Revelation 5:7–8:

> *He came and took the scroll out of the right hand of Him who sat on the throne. When He had taken the scroll, the four living creatures and the twenty-four elders fell down before the Lamb, each one having a harp, and golden bowls full of incense, which are the prayers of saints.*

In the book of Daniel, the angel Gabriel explains to Daniel the meaning of his prayers:

> *While I was speaking and praying and confessing my sin and the sin of my people Israel, and presenting my supplication before the Lord my God for the holy mountain of my God, indeed, while I was speaking in prayer, the man Gabriel, whom I had seen in the vision at the beginning, being caused to fly swiftly, touched me about the time of the evening oblation. He informed me and talked with me, and said, "Daniel, I have now come to give you insight and understanding. At the beginning of your supplications the command went out, and I have come to tell you, for you are greatly beloved. Therefore understand the matter and consider the vision."*
>
> DANIEL 9:20–23

We also find Peter being helped in his release from prison by an angel who was sent in response to prayer. The Bible says "the church prayed to God without ceasing for him" (Acts 12:5). The angel didn't *bring* the answer, in this case, but rather *became* the answer. You can pray this prayer to activate angelic assistance in the realm of prayer.

Angelic Activation Prayer

Father, thank You for your ministering angels. I know my prayers delight You and that You hear my cries. I also know the enemy is opposing my prayer answers, like he did Daniel's, as I fight this good fight of faith (1 Timothy 6:12). I know my prayers are filling up bowls in heaven. I ask You to release angels on assignment to help me in the realm of prayer.

In Jesus' name.

39

ACTIVATING ANGELS OF HEALING

Angels can't heal anyone. Let me repeat that for emphasis: *Angels can't heal anyone.* Angels do not carry God's healing power. They are not partakers of the divine nature. They do not lay hands on the sick and see them recover. That said, God can and does use angels to set the stage for healing.

John 3:3–4 gives us a scriptural precedent for this:

> *In these lay a great crowd of invalids, blind, lame, and paralyzed, waiting for the moving of the water. For an angel went down at a certain time into the pool and stirred up the water. After the stirring of the water, whoever stepped in first was healed of whatever disease he had.*

Although some say this account was not in the original text, most Bibles include it. Voice of Healing prophet William Branham told of an encounter with an angel who helped him in his healing ministry. Here is Branham's account of that angelic visitation, as recorded by the late Gordon Lindsay in his book, *A Man Sent From God.*

> Then alone in the night, at about the eleventh hour, I had quit praying and was sitting up when I noticed a light flickering in the room. Thinking someone was coming with a flashlight, I looked out of the window, but there was no one, and when I looked back, the light was spreading out on the floor, becoming wider. Now I know this seems very strange to you, as it did to me also.
>
> As the light was spreading, of course I became excited and started from the chair, but as I looked up, there hung that great star. However, it did not have five points like a star, but looked more like a ball of fire or light shining down upon the floor. Just then I heard someone walking across the floor, which startled me again, as I knew of no one who would be coming there besides myself. Now, coming through the light, I saw the feet of a man coming toward me, as naturally as you would walk to me.
>
> He appeared to be a man who, in human weight, would weigh about two hundred pounds, clothed in a white robe. He had a smooth face, no beard, dark hair down to his shoulders, rather dark-complexioned, with a very pleasant countenance, and coming closer, his eyes caught with mine. Seeing how fearful I was, he began to speak.
>
> "Fear not. I am sent from the presence of Almighty God to tell you that your peculiar life and your misunderstood ways have been to indicate that God has sent you to take a gift of divine healing to the peoples of the world. IF YOU WILL BE SINCERE, AND CAN GET THE PEOPLE TO BELIEVE YOU, NOTHING SHALL STAND BEFORE YOUR PRAYER, NOT EVEN CANCER."
>
> Words cannot express how I felt. He told me many things, which I do not have space to record here. He told me how I

> would be able to detect diseases by vibrations on my hand. He went away, but I have seen him several times since then. He has appeared to me perhaps once or twice within the space of six months and has spoken with me. A few times he has appeared visibly in the presence of others. I do not know who he is. I only know that he is the messenger of God to me.[110]

I don't believe we should pray for this type of angelic encounter, because the Bible says Satan disguises himself as an angel of light (see 2 Corinthians 11:14). That said, we should be open to anything the Lord wants to do in our lives. Like Mary said when the angel announced she would carry a child called Jesus as the result of an immaculate conception, our heart's cry should be this: "Let be done to me according to thy will, Lord" (see Luke 1:38).

Angelic Activation Prayer

Father, I thank You for Your angels of healing. I thank You that You are a healer and You can send angels to speak to men words of wisdom, words of knowledge, and prophecy that can charge their faith to receive healing. Father, if You want to use me in this capacity, I am open to You. Father, please send angels of healing to help as many people as possible receive Your goodness and grace.

In Jesus' name.

40

Activating Companies of Angels

At times, the Lord may choose to send companies of angels on assignment. This, of course, is His choice. Most of the time when we see angels on assignment in the Bible, we see them flying solo, so to speak. This is especially noteworthy, considering that when Jesus sent His disciples out on assignment, He sent them two by two rather than alone (see Mark 6:7).

There are times when the Lord sends one angel, but then sends a second angel as backup. Daniel 10:13 describes an account in which an angel was sent with prayer answers, but the prince of the kingdom of Persia withstood him twenty-one days. God dispatched Michael, one of the chief princes, to help him overcome.

There are other times we see the Lord dispatching companies of angels on assignment—and suggestions that He could. The Lord has plenty of angels at His disposal, as Hebrews 12:12 tells us:

> *But you have come to Mount Zion and to the city of the living God, the heavenly Jerusalem, and to an innumerable company of angels.*

And John reveals in Revelation 5:11:

> *Then I looked, and I heard around the throne and the living creatures and the elders the voices of many angels, numbering ten thousand times ten thousand, and thousands of thousands.*

Jesus said something telling about angels in the Garden of Gethsemane, in the moment of His betrayal:

> *Then they came and laid hands on Jesus and took Him. Immediately, one of those who were with Jesus stretched out his hand, and drew his sword, and struck the servant of the high priest, and cut off his ear. Then Jesus said to him, "Put your sword back in its place. For all those who take up the sword will perish by the sword. Do you think that I cannot now pray to My Father, and He will at once give Me more than twelve legions of angels?"*
>
> Matthew 26:50–53

What is a legion? According to the KJV New Testament Greek Lexicon, "legion" comes from the Greek word *legeon*. It means "a legion, a body of soldiers whose number differed at different times, and in the time of Augustus seems to have consisted of 6826 men (i.e. 6100 foot soldiers, and 726 horsemen)." Twelve legions of angels would, then, equate to over eighty thousand angels. Now that's an angel army!

God showed Elisha's servant the angel armies that stood with them in 2 Kings 6:15–7:

> *When a servant of the man of God rose early in the morning and went out, a force surrounded the city both with horses and chariots. And his servant said to him, "Alas, my master! What will we do?" And he said, "Do not be afraid, for there are more with us than with them." Then Elisha prayed, "Lord, open his eyes and*

let him see." So the Lord opened the eyes of the young man, and he saw that the mountain was full of horses and chariots of fire surrounding Elisha.

We can activate companies of angels in our lives, but I believe we'd need an unction of the Lord to do so. Jesus chose not to activate twelve legions of angels to save Him from the cross because He knew it was not the Lord's will. There's an important lesson in that: Activating angels should be done in the knowledge of the Lord's will—not in presumption. If you have an unction to release a company of angels—and this may happen during intercessor prayer—you can pray this prayer:

Angelic Activation Prayer

Father, I thank You for your innumerable angels. I thank You, God, that You know when and where to send angels individually, two by two, three by three—in legions, companies, and armies. Father, release your company of nations into my nation, into my city, and into the nations, according to Your will and to do Your will.

In the name of Jesus.

41

Activating Undercover Angels

In some sense, angels on assignment are often undercover. Most of us don't see our angels on assignment. Most of us don't have any idea that angels are among us. They do their work without seeking the praise or applause of men. They refuse to take any glory for themselves, but point people back to God (see Revelation 9:10 and Revelation 22:9).

I am convinced there are undercover angels on assignment that we see with our natural eyes, but that we don't discern with our spirit. Scripture suggests this reality in Hebrews 13:2:

> *Do not forget to entertain strangers, for thereby some have entertained angels unknowingly.*

What does it mean to entertain an angel? The Greek word for "entertain" is *xenzio*, which means "to receive as a guest, to entertain, hospitably; to be received hospitably; to stay as a guest, to lodge; be lodged; to surprise or astonish by the strangeness and novelty of a thing; to think strange, be shocked," according to the KJV New Testament Greek Lexicon.

UNDERCOVER ANGELS MAKE A PROMISE

Abraham and Sarah received the greatest promise of their lives because they entertained an undercover angel. As the account goes, the Lord appeared to Abraham among some oak trees. When he looked up, he saw three men standing in front of him. He ran out to meet them and bowed down to the ground.

> *He said, "My Lord, if I have found favor in Your sight, do not pass by Your servant. Please let a little water be brought and wash your feet and rest yourselves under the tree. I will bring a piece of bread so that you may refresh yourselves. After that you may pass on, now that you have come to your servant."*
>
> GENESIS 18:3–5

The trio of angels took him up on his offer. Abraham told Sarah to cook some food for them quickly as he ran out and selected a calf for his servant to prepare. Then one of the undercover angels shared a prophetic promise that confirmed what the Lord had told Abraham when they had cut covenant:

> *I will certainly return to you about this time next year, and Sarah your wife will have a son.*
>
> GENESIS 18:10

This seemed impossible, since both Abraham and Sarah were so old. In fact, Sarah laughed. But the angels stood on what they knew was the Lord's will:

> *Is anything too difficult for the Lord? At the appointed time I will return to you, at this time next year, and Sarah will have a son.*
>
> GENESIS 18:14

UNDERCOVER ANGELS RESCUE LOT

Lot was careful about entertaining strangers, and it turned out he was entertaining angels.

> *Now the two angels came to Sodom in the evening, and Lot was sitting at the gate of Sodom. When Lot saw them he rose up to meet them, and he bowed himself with his face toward the ground. Then he said, "Here, my lords, please turn in to your servant's house and spend the night and wash your feet; and then you may rise early and go on your way."*
>
> GENESIS 19:1–2

It is not clear whether Lot knew these were angels. But he brought them into his house, set a feast before them, and protected them. In turn, the angels protected Lot, his wife, and his daughters from destruction when the Lord rained fire and brimstone down on Sodom and Gomorrah to destroy the sinful cities. Lot's willingness to entertain angels saved his life. We can ask the Lord to give us discernment regarding undercover angels He may send us to entertain—and to help us.

Angelic Activation Prayer

Father, thank You for Your mighty angels on assignment to minister to me. Please give me discernment to recognize angels who come in the form of strangers. Help me to rightly entertain them that I might receive the benefit of their ministry.

In Jesus' name.

42

Activating Church Angels

Although some may argue with this interpretation, the book of Revelation suggests there are angels who are assigned to specific churches. Revelation 1:20 states:

> *The mystery of the seven stars which you saw in My right hand, and the seven golden candlesticks: The seven stars are the angels of the seven churches, and the seven candlesticks which you saw are the seven churches.*

We see the angels of the seven churches mentioned in the following Scriptures:

- Revelation 2:1—The angel of the church of Ephesus
- Revelation 2:8—The angel of the church of Smyrna
- Revelation 2:12—The angel of the church of Pergamum

- Revelation 2:18—The angel of the church of Thyatira
- Revelation 3:1—The angel of the church of Sardis
- Revelation 3:7—The angel of the church of Philadelphia
- Revelation 3:14—The angel of the church of Laodicea

The Holy Spirit inspired John to write a letter to the angels of each of these churches. In all but two letters, Jesus offered not only praise but also rebuke. Do churches have angels? I believe they do. Some argue that these angels were the pastors of the church. The Greek word for "angel" and "angels" in these verses is *aggelos*, which means "a messenger, envoy, one who is sent, an angel, a messenger from God," according to the KJV New Testament Greek Lexicon. Could this be the leader of the church? It's very possible, yet still debated.

I believe churches do have angels assigned to them—more than one. First Timothy 5:21 seems to offer proof:

> *I command you before God and the Lord Jesus Christ and the elect angels that you observe these things without prejudice, doing nothing by partiality.*

In 1 Corinthians 11:10, Paul seems to point out that angels are watching what happens in the local church:

> *For this reason the woman ought to have a veil of authority over her head, because of the angels.*

It's likely that angels assigned to your church are activated in some sense, but they harken to the Word of God (see Psalm 103:20). I believe that when we confess, decree, declare, and proclaim God's Word over our churches, it fuels the elect angels.

Angelic Activation Prayer

Father, I thank You for Your elect angels. Thank You for sending angels on assignment in my church to protect, guard, reveal, and perform other functions. I stand in agreement with Your angels on assignment. Give me a discerning spirit that I might not hinder their work in this local body.

In Jesus' name.

43

Activating Proclaiming Angels

Although the Lord will lead us to proclaim a thing, He also sends angels on assignment to proclaim His will on the earth. This angelic function is especially prevalent in the end times, as we see two strong examples worth noting in the book of Revelation:

> *Then I saw in the right hand of Him who sat on the throne a scroll written within and on the back, sealed with seven seals. And I saw a strong angel proclaiming with a loud voice, "Who is worthy to open the scroll and to break its seals?" But no one in heaven or on earth or under the earth was able to open the scroll or to look in it.*
>
> Revelation 5:1–3

The Greek word for "proclaim" in this verse is *kerusso*, which means: "to be a herald, to officiate as a herald; to proclaim after the manner of a herald; always with the suggestion of formality, gravity and an authority which must be listened to and obeyed; to publish, proclaim openly: something which has been done used of the public proclamation of the gospel and matters pertaining to it, made by John the Baptist, by Jesus, by the apostles and other Christian teachers," according to the *KJV New Testament Greek Lexicon.*

We also see angels proclaiming victory in Revelation 14:8:

> *Another angel followed, saying, "Fallen! Fallen is Babylon, that Great City," because she made all the nations drink of the wine of the wrath of her sexual immorality.*

A question that arises is this: What is the difference between our proclamations and angelic proclamations? One difference is that angels are sent on assignment with specific proclamations during specific times and seasons. Angels don't just decide what and when to make a proclamation. Remember, they harken to the voice of God's word (see Psalm 103:20).

By contrast, believers may proclaim the Word of God—the will of God—which is Scripture at any given moment by the authority of Jesus. Believers can make proclamations based on faith alone without any particular unction of the Holy Spirit. For example, we can proclaim healing because we know it's the Lord's will to heal. We don't have to have a special leading of the Spirit to proclaim what we know is God's will.

That said, when we make proclamations under the anointing by the leading of the Spirit, I believe there is a greater degree of supernatural power released into any given situation that the Lord wants to address. The Bible says the words God speaks will not return void (see Isaiah 55:11).

Believers, too, can fall into a measure of presumption, proclaiming the wrong Scripture into the wrong situation with the wrong motive. God is not obliged to breathe life into a proclamation that is rooted in fleshly desires or that perverts or twists the intent of Scripture. Proclaiming angels on assignment do not make this mistake, because God's holy angels only speak what they hear God say. They don't presume to make proclamations apart from their God-given assignment.

God can choose to send a proclaiming angel into our lives. We can also proclaim His Word out our own mouths. Hebrews 4:12 reveals:

> *For the Word that God speaks is alive and full of power [making it active, operative, energizing, and effective]; it is sharper than any two-edged sword, penetrating to the dividing line of the breath of life (soul) and [the immortal] spirit, and of joints and marrow [of the deepest parts of our nature], exposing and sifting and analyzing and judging the very thoughts and purposes of the heart.*

As I write in my book, *Waging Prophetic Warfare*:

> When you proclaim the Word of God over your life, the Holy Spirit can breathe on a situation. The writer of Hebrews calls God's Word "powerful." When you declare the Word during spiritual warfare, it has vital power to bring itself to pass. In other words, the power necessary to accomplish God's declared Word is contained in the Word itself. Words are like containers of power, and carry the power of death and life (see Proverbs 18:21).
>
> But that's not all. The Word of God is also sharp. In fact, it's sharper than any two-edged sword. That means your Sword of the Spirit, which is the Word of God, can cut through any weapon that's formed against you. That's why God can so confidently declare that those weapons cannot prosper. This truth is part of our spiritual heritage (see Isaiah 54:17). Finally, God's Word pierces, or penetrates, the darkness. The unfolding of His Word gives light (see Psalm 119:30) and darkness has to flee when that Word is declared in faith. The Father of lights enforces His Word.

I believe angels of proclamation back up our proclamations. You can pray this prayer when you feel you need angelic backup on a Spirit-inspired proclamation.

Angelic Activation Prayer

Father, in the name of Jesus, I thank You for Your Word. It's alive. Jesus is alive. It's sharp. It doesn't return to You void. Father, I am asking you to send proclaiming angels on assignment to proclaim in the heavens what I am proclaiming on the earth and what you have already proclaimed in heaven. Let Your kingdom come and Your will be done, on earth as it is in heaven.

In the name of Your Son Jesus.

44

Activating Angels of the Waters

Angels of the waters are not a category we hear much about. We discover these heavenly beings in Revelation 16:5:

> *Then I heard the angel of the waters saying: "You are righteous, O Lord, who is and was and who is to be, because You have judged these things."*

Who are angels of the waters? The Greek word for "waters" in this verse is *hudor*. It means "water; of water in rivers, in fountains, in pools of the water of the deluge; of water in any of the earth's repositories; of water as the primary element, out of and through which the world that was before the deluge, arose and was compacted; of the waves of the sea fig. used of many peoples," according to the *KJV New Testament Greek Lexicon*.

Barnes' *Notes on the Bible* reveals this is "the angel who presides over the element of water; in allusion to the common opinion among the

Hebrews that the angels presided over elements, and that each element was committed to the jurisdiction of a particular angel."

In spiritual warfare circles, we believe in water spirits—including python and leviathan. It stands to reason that if there are demon spirits over waters, there are angels over waters. It's possible that the angel who troubled the water in John 5 was an angel of the water.

Whether for healing, help in spiritual warfare, restoration of water sources, or any other purpose, our prayer should be to the Creator of the Universe—the creator of the seas, the rivers, and all waters. The Lord may choose to send angels of the water, though, and we can activate them at his leading.

Angelic Activation

Father, I thank You that You created all things. You created the land and the seas by Your Word, and You have given me authority in this earth. In the name of Jesus, I command the waters in my community to be healed. I command the evil water spirits in my area to be bound. I thank You, Lord, for sending your angels on assignment to contend in the waters.

In Jesus' name.

45

Questions and Answers about Angels on Assignment

Throughout the pages of this book, we've posed many questions and offered some answers scripturally and from experts who have encountered angels. Yet many questions remain. In this final chapter, we'll explore some questions we didn't answer in this book but that are arousing the curiosity of many who believe angels are on assignment.

While on assignment, do angels speak to one another?

The Bible speaks of tongues of angels (1 Corinthians 13:1), so do angels on assignment speak to one another as they execute the will of the Lord? Nowhere in Scripture do we actually see angels communicating with one another—but we do see them worshipping, crying out with a loud voice, proclaiming and speaking to humans. It is clear that angels have the ability to communicate and must communicate with one another. How they communicate with one another while on assignment remains a hidden mystery.

What are tongues of angels?

First Corinthians 13:1 says:

> *If I speak with the tongues of men and of angels, and have not love, I have become as sounding brass or a clanging cymbal."*

The Greek word for tongue in this verse is *glossa*, which in this context means "the language or dialect used by a particular people distinct from that of other nations," according to the *KJV New Testament Lexicon*. There is much debate over what is meant by "tongues of angels." What we do know is that in the Bible angels speak to men in a language they understand. While on assignment to interact with humans, they speak our language.

Do angels on assignment speak to God?

Angels do speak to God. We see Lucifer, a fallen angel, speaking to God in the book of Job. The account is in Job 1:6–12 before Job's trials began:

> *Now there was a day when the sons of God came to present themselves before the Lord, and the Adversary also came among them. And the Lord said to the Adversary, "From where have you come?" Then the Adversary answered the Lord, saying, "From roaming on the earth, and from walking up and down on it." And the Lord said to the Adversary, "Have you considered My servant Job, that there is none like him on the earth, a blameless and an upright man, who fears God, and avoids evil?"*
>
> *Then the Adversary answered the Lord, saying, "Has Job feared God for nothing? Have You not made a hedge around him, around his household, and around all that he has on every side? You have blessed the work of his hands, and his possessions have increased in the land. But stretch out Your hand now, and touch all that he has,*

and he will curse You to Your face." The Lord said to the Adversary, "Look, all that he has is in your power; only do not stretch out your hand against his person." So the Adversary departed from the presence of the Lord.

In a separate instance, we see an angel speaking to the Lord. We find this account in Zechariah 1:12–15:

Then the angel of the Lord said, "How much longer, O Lord of Hosts, will You withhold mercy from Jerusalem and the cities of Judah with which You have been angry these seventy years?" And the Lord answered the angel speaking to me with good and comforting words. So the angel who spoke with me said, "Cry out, saying: Thus says the Lord of Hosts: I have a great jealousy for Jerusalem and Zion. And I have a great anger for those nations who are at ease, for while I was angry but a little, they helped to increase evil."

Can angels on assignment perform miracles?

We see nowhere in Scripture where angels actually perform miracles. That said, angels seem to set the stage for miracles according to John 5:3–4:

In these lay a great crowd of invalids, blind, lame, and paralyzed, waiting for the moving of the water. For an angel went down at a certain time into the pool and stirred up the water. After the stirring of the water, whoever stepped in first was healed of whatever disease he had.

We know that Satan, who disguises himself as an angel of light (see 2 Corinthians 11:14) is connected to the lawless one mentioned in 2 Thessalonians 2:9–10:

> *Him, whose coming is in accordance with the working of Satan with all power and signs and false wonders, and with all deception of unrighteousness among those who perish, because they did not receive the love for the truth that they might be saved.*

Do angels on assignment fly?

Although not all angels have wings, the Bible does speak of angels that fly. Angels, however, don't necessarily need wings in order to fly. John saw angels flying in the book of Revelation. Here are two accounts:

Revelation 8:13:

> *Then I watched, and I heard an angel flying through the midst of heaven, saying with a loud voice, "Woe, woe, woe to the inhabitants of the earth, because of the other trumpet blasts of the three angels, who are yet to sound!"*

Revelation 14:6:

> *Then I saw another angel flying in the midst of heaven, having the eternal gospel to preach to those who dwell on the earth, to every nation and tribe and tongue and people.*

While on assignment, angels can move quickly—and even fly.

Do angels on assignment know everything?

Angels have an intellect but they are not omniscient. Only God is omniscient. His understanding is infinite (Psalm 147:5). For example, Matthew 24:36 tells us with regard to the Second Coming of Christ:

Concerning that day and hour no one knows, not even the angels of heaven, but My Father only. As were the days of Noah, so will be the coming of the Son of Man.

And angels desire to look into issues such as man's salvation:

Concerning this salvation, the prophets who prophesied of the grace that should come to you have inquired and searched diligently, seeking the events and time the Spirit of Christ, who was within them, signified when He foretold the sufferings of Christ and the glories to follow. It was revealed to them that they were not serving themselves but you, concerning the things which are now reported to you by those who have preached the gospel to you through the Holy Spirit, who was sent from heaven—things into which the angels desire to look.

1 Peter 1:10–12

Angels don't know everything, but they take direct orders from the all-knowing God at all times.

Do angels on assignment have discernment?

Yes, angels have discernment. When Joab was working to get Absalom back into King David's presence after he killed his brother, he sent a woman undercover to the palace. She was pretending to be grieving over the loss of her son and shared her cause for David to judge. As part of that conversation, she said:

For like the angel of God, my lord the king discerns good from evil.

2 Samuel 14:17

Angels can discern good from evil, and need this ability on assignment.

Do angels carry wisdom in their assignment?

Yes, Scripture speaks of the wisdom of the angel of God (2 Samuel 14:20). The Hebrew word for "wisdom" is *chokmah*, which means "wisdom," according to the *KJV Old Testament Hebrew Lexicon*. But the lexicon breaks it down into categories, which offers more insight into the intellect and wisdom of angels: skill (in war); wisdom (in administration); shrewdness, wisdom; wisdom, prudence (in religious affairs); wisdom (ethical and religious). God has granted angels wisdom, which is helpful as they execute their God-given assignment.

Are all angels sent on assignment?

It seems all angels have an assignment of some sort. Some find their place in heaven worshipping the Lord. Others seem to ascend and descend. Still others are warring angels. God did not make creatures to sit idle. Every angel has a purpose and a function in the kingdom of God. Likewise, the devil sends his minions on assignment.

Can prophetic revelation come through angels on assignment?

Yes, we see angels who bring messages in dreams and open visions to people God chooses. Daniel receives interpretations to his dreams. In the book of Revelation, angels explain to John what he is seeing in a vision Zechariah also receive angelic assistance in the prophetic realm.

Will God send angels on assignment to judge in the end times?

Angels will execute God's judgment. We see this as a running theme in the book of Revelation. But will not in themselves judge. Believers will judge angels. First Corinthians 6:3 says, "Do you not know that we shall judge angels?"

The Greek word for "judge" is *krino*, which in this context means "to pronounce an opinion concerning right and wrong to be judged, i.e. summoned to trial that one's case may be examined and judgment passed upon it to pronounce judgment, to subject to censure of those who act the part of judges or arbiters in matters of common life, or pass judgment on the deeds and words of others to rule, govern."

Can angels on assignment change man's will?

No, angels cannot change man's will. Demons can influence man to change his will, but nobody can change man's will. God cannot even change man's will. He has given us a free will. We can, for example, choose to obey or disobey God's commands (see Deuteronomy 30:19).

Can angels on assignment influence man's imagination?

We know Satan's angels can influence our imagination, so it stands to reason that God's angels could influence our mind by what they speak on His behalf.

Speaking to the Pharisees, Jesus exposed a spiritual truth about the nature of the enemy that suggests the enemy can whisper lies that impact our mind:

> *You are of your father the devil, and you want to do the desires of your father. He was a murderer from the beginning, and does not stand in the truth, because there is no truth in him. When he lies, he speaks from his own nature, for he is a liar and the father of lies.*
>
> JOHN 8:44

Second Corinthians 10:5 tells us:

> *...casting down imaginations and every high thing that exalts itself against the knowledge of God, bringing every thought into captivity to the obedience of Christ.*

God does not want us to cast down the imaginations he gives us. He wants us to cast down the imaginations—some translations say arguments—of demonic powers.

Can angels on assignment sin?

It seems angels were created with a free will, since one-third of the angels in heaven followed Lucifer in the insurrection. Jude 20 explains:

> *Likewise, the angels who did not keep to their first domain, but forsook their own dwelling, He has kept in everlasting chains under darkness for the judgment of the great day.*

Some argue that there came a point when the angels were "elected" as holy and cannot sin.

Do angels have any emotion about or during their assignments?

It seems angels do have emotions. Luke 15:10 tells us:

> *Likewise, I tell you, there is joy in the presence of the angels of God over one sinner who repents.*

If angels can rejoice, they can grieve. It seems what grieves the Lord grieves angels.

Can bad angels—demons—hinder angels on assignment?

Yes, we read of one such instance in Daniel 10:10–14:

> *But then a hand touched me, which set me on my knees and on the palms of my hands. He said to me, "O Daniel, a man greatly beloved, understand the words that I speak to you, and stand upright, for I have been sent to you now." And when he had spoken this word to me, I stood trembling.*
>
> *Then he said to me, "Do not be afraid, Daniel. For from the first day that you set your heart to understand this and to humble yourself before your God, your words were heard, and I have come because of your words. But the prince of the kingdom of Persia withstood me for twenty-one days. So Michael, one of the chief princes, came to help me, for I had been left there with the kings of Persia. Now I have come to make you understand what shall befall your people in the latter days. For the vision is yet for many days."*

Can demons on assignment to hinder us succeed?

It seems so. Paul's endeavors to visit the church at Thessalonica fell flat. Paul writes:

> *Therefore we wanted to come to you—even I, Paul, time and again—but Satan hindered us.*
>
> 1 Thessalonians 2:18

We don't know exactly how Paul determined it was Satan hindering him rather than the Holy Spirit preventing him or what Satan may have done to hinder him. But Paul was certain the devil was to blame.

Can angels be assigned to nations?

This seems possible. Some would say that Michael is a defender of Israel. Daniel 10:13 suggests this:

> *But the prince of the kingdom of Persia withstood me for twenty-one days. So Michael, one of the chief princes, came to help me, for I had been left there with the kings of Persia.*

And Daniel 10:20 offers more evidence:

> *Then he said, "Do you understand why I have come to you? But now I shall return to fight against the prince of Persia, and when I have gone forth, then truly the prince of Greece will come."*

Will angels on assignment help Jesus at His Second Coming?

Angels will accompany Jesus in His Second Coming. Matthew 25:31 declares:

> *When the Son of Man comes in His glory, and all the holy angels with Him, then He will sit on the throne of His glory.*

What is Satan's main assignment?

Jesus reveals Satan's overall assignment—and the general assignment of every demon following him—in John 10:10:

> *The thief does not come, except to steal and kill and destroy. I came that they may have life, and that they may have it more abundantly.*

The enemy may work to steal, kill, and destroy in many ways, but that's his three-fold ministry.

Can angels be assigned to churches?

Yes, we see angels assigned to churches in the book of Revelation.

What are some of the assignments of angels in heaven?

Angels in heaven praise God (see Job 1:6 and Job 6:2). Angels in heaven share in God's joy over salvation (see Luke 15:7). Angels in heaven stand in the presence of God (see Matthew 18:10).

What are the names of angels on assignment in the Bible?

The Bible only names five angels. In alphabetical order, those are: Abaddon, Beelzebul, Gabriel, Michael, and Satan. Two of these are holy angels. Three are fallen angels. Let's look at each of these angels on assignment:

Apollyon: Also called Abaddon, this is the angel of the bottomless pit found in the book of Revelation. Revelation 9:11 reads:

> *They had as king over them the angel of the bottomless pit, whose name in Hebrew is Abaddon, and in Greek his name is Apollyon.*

We find Abaddon mentioned three other times in Scripture: Psalm 88:1; Proverbs 15:11; and Proverbs 27:20. Abaddon is a dark place of torment.

Beelzebub: Also called Beelzebul, the name literally means "lord of the flies." This is a false god whose name we see rise up in the both the Old and New Testaments. We can read verses about him in 2 Kings 1:2; 2 Kings 1:16; Matthew 10:25; Matthew 12:24; Mark 3:22; and Luke 11:15.

Gabriel: Gabriel is a carrier of messages in the Bible. We see him on assignment in Daniel 8:16, Daniel 9:21, Luke 1:19 and Luke 1:26.

Michael: Michael is a warring angel. We see him on assignment in Daniel 10:13, Daniel 12:1, Jude 9, and Revelation 12:7–8.

Satan: Once called Lucifer, Satan's operations are found throughout the New Testament. Some Scriptures include Matthew 4:10, Mark 1:13, Luke 22:3, Romans 16:20, and Revelation 12:9.

How else are angels on assignment referred to in the Bible?

Angel of the Lord—Some debate this is God Himself (see Matthew 1:20; Luke 1:11; and Acts 5:19).

Angels of God—These are seen in Genesis 32:1.

Archangels—These are mentioned in 1 Thessalonians 4:16. Michael and Gabriel are archangels.

Cherubim—These are mentioned in Genesis 3:34.

Heavenly Host—These are found in Nehemiah 9:6, Colossians 1:16, and Luke 2:13–14.

Morning Stars—These are revealed in Job 38:7

Principalities—These are discovered in Romans 8:38 and Ephesians 6.

Rulers and Authorities—These are found in Ephesians 3:10 and again in Colossians 1:16.

Seraphim—These are featured in Isaiah 6:2.

Seven Stars—These are seen in Revelation 1:20.

Sons of God—These are talked about in Job 1:6.

Star of the Morning—This is a name used in Isaiah 14:12.

Watchers—These are discovered in Daniel 4:17.

Can angels on assignment die?

No, angels cannot die. Luke 20:36 tells us:

For they cannot die any more, for they are equal to the angels and are the sons of God, being sons of the resurrection.

Angels are eternal beings that do not die.

Who gives angels their marching orders?

God commands angels. Humans do not command angels. Psalm 103:20 tells us:

Bless the Lord, you His angels, who are mighty, and do His commands, and obey the voice of His word.

The New Living Translation of that verse reads:

Praise the Lord, you angels, you mighty ones who carry out his plans, listening for each of his commands.

And The Message translation reads:

Bless God, all you armies of angels, alert to respond to whatever he wills. Bless God, all creatures, wherever you are—everything and everyone made by God.

Jesus is the head of the angels now. Second Thessalonians 1:7 speaks of Jesus and His powerful angels. Matthew 24:31 tells us Jesus will send out His angels with the mighty blast of a trumpet. If Jesus is the head of all principalities and powers—and He is—then He is also in charge of the angels (see Colossians 2:10).

46

A Dictionary of Angels

Angel: From the Greek word *aggelos*, an angel is a messenger. It's a masculine noun that means "a messenger, generally a (supernatural) messenger from God, an angel, conveying news or behests from God to men," according to Strong's Concordance. From the Hebrew word *malak*, a masculine noun for angel.

Angels of announcement: Some angels are on assignment with prophetic announcements. Angels announced the birth of John the Baptist and Jesus. (See Matthew 1:20–21; Luke 1:11–13.)

Angel of the bottomless pit: Also known as Apollyon or Abaddon (see Revelation 9:11), this is a dark angel on assignment who will battle Michael and his angels (see Revelation 12:7–9).

Angels of the churches: These are angels on assignment over the various churches in the book of Revelation (see Revelation 1:20; Revelation 2:1, 8, 12, 18; Revelation 3:1, 7, 14).

Angels of direction: These are angels on assignment to help direct people. (See Genesis 24:1–7; Acts 8:26.)

Angels of deliverance: These are angels on assignment to deliver us from dangerous situations (Acts 5:19; Acts 12:7–11).

Angels of destruction: These are angels God sends on assignment for destructive purposes. (See Genesis 19:13 ; 2 Samuel 24:16 ; 2 Kings 19:35, etc.)

Angels of fire: These angels can minister the fire of God to prepare and empower believers for the work of the ministry. (See Psalm 104:4; Hebrews 1:7; Acts 2:3.)

Angelic hosts: These heavenly hosts are on assignment to praise God day and night. (See 1 Kings 22:19; Psalm 103:21.)

Angels of interpretation: These are angels with the assignment to help interpret God-given dreams. (See Daniel 7:16; Daniel 10:5.)

Angels of judgment: These are angels on assignment on the end-times to execute judgment. (See Revelation 7:1; Revelation 8:2.)

Angels of promise: These angels on assignment deliver or remind us of the promises of God (see Genesis 16:6–10).

Angels of provision: These angels on assignment bring the Lord's provision. (See Genesis 21:15–19; 1 Kings 19:5–6.)

Angels of rebuke: These angels are sent on assignment with a word of rebuke to correct people on their path. (See Numbers 22:22–23.)

Angels of revelation: God sends these angels on assignment to bring revelation to His people. (See Acts 8:26–27; Acts 27:23–24; Daniel 9:21–22.)

Angels of transition: These angels help believers transition to the next place God is taking them. The Holy Spirit leads and guides us, but ministering spirits can minister to believers in times of transition, even into heaven (see Luke 16:22).

Angels of warning: While the Holy Spirit warns us of impending danger, God can send these angels on assignment to warn us of situations and circumstances we need to avoid and even show us the way of escape. (See Genesis 19:1–10.)

Archangels: These are princes of angels in the hierarchy of angels (see Colossians 1:15–18; 1 Thessalonians 4:16; Jude 9).

Cherubim: These are winged creatures (Exodus 25:20); they expelled Adam and Eve from the Garden of Eden (Genesis 3:24).

Demons: These are evil spirits roaming the earth under Satan's command (Luke 4:35; Luke 11:15; John 10:21).

Fallen angels: These angels followed Lucifer's coup and were expelled from heaven.

Forerunner angels: These angels are assigned to go before us to make a way for us (see Exodus 23:23).

Guardian angels: Also called angels of protection, these ministering spirits are sent on assignment to guard and protect believers (Matthew 18:10; Acts 12:15).

Harvesting angels: These are angels with an assignment to help bring in the harvest (see Acts 8:23; Acts 10:3).

Healing angels: God sends these angels on assignment at times to assist in healing ministry (see John 5:4).

Messenger angels: These are angels, such as Gabriel, who bring messages (see Luke 31).

Prayer angels: These angels are assigned to bring prayer answers (see Daniel 9:21–31; Daniel 10:12–13).

Reassuring angels: These angels that bring us reassurance in times of stress (see Luke 2:10).

Seraphim: These are winged creatures seated above God's throne (see Isaiah 6:1–2).

Strengthening angels: These angels come to strengthen God's people (Luke 22:40–44).

Watcher angels: These are angels whose assignment is to watch and record what people do (Malachi 3:6).

Warring angels: These angels are on assignment to war with and for us against dark forces. (See 2 Kings 19:35.)

Worshipping angels: These angels are on assignment to worship God. (See Isaiah 6:30.)

Wicked angels: These angels are on a wicked assignment for Satan (2 Peter, Jude).

NOTES

1. "The AP-Gfk Poll: December 2011," *Associated Press*, last accessed May 2, 2017, http://surveys.ap.org/data/GfK/AP-GfK%20Poll%20December%202011%20Topline_Santa.pdf.
2. "Majority of Americans Surveyed Believe Heaven and Hell Exist, the Devil and Angels Are Real and God Is Not Responsible for Recent U.S. Tragedies," *PR Newswire*, from "True Life in God Foundation Poll," last accessed May 2, 2017, http://www.prnewswire.com/news-releases/majority-of-americans-surveyed-believe-heaven-and-hell-exist-the-devil-and-angels-are-real-and-god-is-not-responsible-for-recent-us-tragedies-209383941.html.
3. "Belief in Angels," *The Association of Religious Data Archives*, last accessed May 2, 2017, http://www.thearda.com/quickstats/qs_74.asp.
4. "Belief in Demons," *The Association of Religious Data Archives*, last accessed May 2, 2017, http://www.thearda.com/quickstats/qs_75.asp.
5. "U.S. Religious Landscape Survey: Summary of Findings" *Pew Forum on Religion & Public Life*, last accessed May 2, 2017, http://www.pewforum.org/files/2008/06/report2religious-landscape-study-key-findings.pdf.
6. "Baylor Survey Finds New Perspectives on U.S. Religious Landscape," *Baylor*, last accessed May 2, 2017, http://www.baylor.edu/mediacommunications/news.php?action=story&story=52815.
7. Jay Schadler and Harry Phillips, "Do Guardian Angels Exist? Investigating Our Invisible Companions," April 27, 2013, *ABC News*, last accessed May 2, 2017, http://abcnews.go.com/US/guardian-angels-exist-investigating-invisible-companions/story?id=19053535.
8. Ibid.

9. "Does the Belief in Guardian Angels Make People More Cautious?" September 23, 2014, *EurekAlert*, from *SAGE*, last accessed May 2, 2017, https://www.eurekalert.org/pub_releases/2014-09/sp-dtb091914.php.
10. Ibid.
11. Shweta Iyer, "Belief in Guardian Angels Makes People More Cautious: Survey," September 23, 2014, *Medical Daily*, last accessed May 2, 2017, http://www.medicaldaily.com/belief-guardian-angels-makes-people-more-cautious-survey-304426.
12. "U.S. Religious Landscape Survey," *Pew Forum*.
13. "Angels," *New Advent Catholic Encyclopedia*, last accessed May 2, 2017, http://www.newadvent.org/cathen/01476d.htm.
14. "Angels," *The Church of Jesus Christ of Latter-Day Saints Dictionary Online*, last accessed May 2, 2017, https://www.lds.org/scriptures/bd/angels.html?lang=eng&letter=A.
15. "Varieties of Angels and Demons in the Religions of the World," *Encyclopaedia Britannica*, last accessed May 2, 2017, https://www.britannica.com/topic/angel-religion/Varieties-of-angels-and-demons-in-the-religions-of-the-world.
16. Ibid.
17. Ibid.
18. Ibid.
19. Ibid.
20. Billy Graham, "Answers," May 11, 2005, *Billy Graham Evangelical Association*, last accessed May 2, 2017, https://billygraham.org/answer/when-were-the-angels-created-3/.
21. Ibid.
22. Audrey Wilson, "Big in Thailand: Fake Kids," May 2016 issue of *The Atlantic*, last accessed May 2, 2017, https://www.theatlantic.com/magazine/archive/2016/05/big-inthailand-fake-children/476400/.
23. Cover of *Time Magazine* can be found at the following URL, last accessed May 2, 2017: http://content.time.com/time/covers/0,16641,19931227,00.html.

24. David Van Biema, "Guardian Angels Are Here, Say Most Americans," September 18, 2008, *Time Magazine Online*, last accessed May 2, 2017, http://content.time.com/time/nation/article/0,8599,1842179,00.html.
25. Brie Schwartz, "Is There an Angel Protecting the Baby in This Ultrasound?" January 6, 2016, *Redbook*, last accessed May 2, 2017, http://www.redbookmag.com/life/news/a41852/sonogram-angel-ultrasound/.
26. Ron Rhodes, "Close Encounters of the Celestial Kind: Evaluating Today's Angel Craze," *Reasoning from the Scriptures Ministries*, last accessed May 2, 2017, http://home.earthlink.net/~ronrhodes/AngelsArticle.html.
27. Dr. John Ankerberg and Dr. John Weldon, "What's Behind the Sudden Craze Over Angels?" 2004, *John Ankerberg Show*, last accessed May 2, 2017, https://www.jashow.org/articles/bible/angels/whats-behind-the-sudden-craze-over-angels/.
28. Diane Swanbrow, "The History of Angels: U-M Research," November 15, 2011, *Michigan News*, last accessed May 2, 2017, http://www.ns.umich.edu/new/releases/20064-the-history-of-angels-u-m-research.
29. Ibid.
30. Ibid.
31. Ibid.
32. Show description can be found at the following URL, last accessed May 2, 2017, http://www.cbs.com/shows/touched-by-an-angel/.
33. Show description can be found at the following URL, last accessed May 2, 2017, http://lucifer.wikia.com/wiki/File:Charlotte_Goes_To_Linda_For_Advice_Season_2_Ep._12_LUCIFER.
34. Luke Morgan Britton, "Florence Welch 'Almost Wrote a Concept Album about the LA Witchcraft Scene,'" June 3, 2015, *NME*, last accessed May 2, 2017, http://www.nme.com/news/music/florence-and-the-machine-52-1211447#827CDlYMQxeDorhr.99.
35. Samuel C. Baxter, "Magic, Horror and the Occult—Why the

Attraction?" *Real Truth*, last accessed May 2, 2017, https://realtruth.org/articles/121030-001.html.

36. Ibid.
37. "New Research Explores Teenage Views and Behavior Regarding the Supernatural," January 23, 2006, *Barna Group*, last accessed May 2, 2017, https://www.barna.com/research/new-research-explores-teenage-views-and-behavior-regarding-the-supernatural/#.
38. Book description can be found at the following URL, last accessed May 2, 2017, https://www.amazon.com/Name-Your-Demon-Dima-Zales/dp/1539363600.
39. To observe the effects of Led Zepplin's "Stairway to Heaven" in reverse, see the following URL, last accessed May 2, 2017, http://www.albinoblacksheep.com/flash/stairway.
40. Lyrics available here: http://www.azlyrics.com/lyrics/eminem/the-monster.html, last accessed May 2, 2017.
41. Lyrics available here: http://www.azlyrics.com/lyrics/imaginedragons/demons.html, last accessed May 2, 2017.
42. Jessica Schladebeck, "Beyoncé Accidentally Rips Off Earring and Bleeds Onstage...WARNING GRAPHIC CONTENT," October 17, 2006, *NYDaily News*, last accessed May 2, 2017, http://www.nydailynews.com/entertainment/beyonce-bleeds-stage-fans-cut-solidarity-article-1.2833600.
43. Ibid.
44. "Do You Believe? Holy Image Appears Behind Child Battling Leukemia," May 24, 2013, *Fox News*, last accessed May 2, 2017, http://www.kptv.com/story/22416520/do-you-believe-holy-image-appears-behind-child-battling-leukemia.
45. Mike Celizic, "Did an Angel Save Girl from Dying in Hospital?," December 23, 2008, *Today Show*, last accessed May 2, 2017, http://www.today.com/id/28364813/ns/today-today_news/t/did-angel-save-girl-dying-hospital/#.WPiYtFPyvjA.
46. Joe Kovacs, "'Angel' Caught on Home-Security Camera," August 26, 2013, *World Net Daily*, last accessed May 2, 2017, http://www.wnd.com/2013/08/christian-minister-catches-angel-on-camera/#CEofbbRGDgLdZbVv.99.

47. Sarah Buchanan, "Saintly Sighting of Angel of the South Spotted Hovering Above Stonehenge," October 8, 2014, *Express*, last accessed May 2, 2017, http://www.express.co.uk/news/weird/520241/Angel-South-spotted-Stonehenge-Toby-Elles.
48. Laura Santos, Angel in Sky Photos: South Florida Sees a Message from Above," March 13, 2013, *WPTV*, last accessed May 2, 2017, http://www.wptv.com/news/region-c-palm-beach-county/west-palm-beach/a-message-from-above.
49. Lillie Leonardi, *In the Shadow of a Badge: A Memoir About Flight 93, a Field of Angels, and My Spiritual Homecoming* (World Association Publishers, 2001), 20–21.
50. Matt Blake, "'The Angel of 9/11': Haunting Face Appears in Mangled Girder Taken from the EXACT Spot Where the First Plane Smashed into the Twin Towers," December 2, 2013, *Daily Mail*, last accessed May 2, 2017, http://www.dailymail.co.uk/news/article-2517002/The-Angel-9-11-Haunting-face-appears-mangled-girder-taken-EXACT-spot-plane-smashed-Twin-Towers.html.
51. "What Is the Eerie Noise Coming from One World Trade Center? 'Unmistakable and Very Chilling' Recording Captures a Sound that has Baffled New Yorkers since Last Year," December 3, 2013, *Daily Mail*, last accessed May 2, 2017, http://www.dailymail.co.uk/news/article-2517472/What-eerie-noise-coming-World-Trade-Center.html.
52. Joe Kovacs, "Angels Singing Caught on Tape?" February 18, 2007, *World Net Daily*, last accessed May 2, 2017, http://www.wnd.com/2007/02/40193/#2GzUbTTXYo7AOYkh.99.
53. Ibid.
54. Norman Byrd, "UFO Over Washington, D.C., After Election: Video of 'Angel' a 'Blessing From God' for Trump?" November 10, 2016, *Inquisitr*, last accessed May 2, 2017, http://www.inquisitr.com/3703443/ufo-over-washington-dc-after-election-video-of-angel-a-blessing-from-god-for-trump/?utm_source=feedburner&utm_medium=feed&utm_campaign=Feed%3A+google%2FyDYq+%28The+Inquisitr+-+News%29.

55. Charlie Moore, "Video Captures Mysterious Bright White UFO 'Shaped Like an Angel' in the Skies Over Alicante," May 6, 2016, *Daily Mail*, last accessed May 2, 2017, http://www.dailymail.co.uk/news/article-3577878/Video-captures-mysterious-bright-white-UFO-shaped-like-angel-skies-Alicante.html#ixzz4en8NQ29J.
56. "UFO Overtakes Blue Angels at Full Vertical Climb," YouTube video, uploaded by UFO News on April 23, 2016, last accessed May 2, 2017, https://www.youtube.com/watch?v=3JlfNPKKa7w.
57. Kayla Rodgers, "A Clip of a Cloud Shaped Like an 'Angel' Has the Web Abuzz," October 20, 2016, *CNN News*, last accessed May 2, 2017, http://www.cnn.com/2016/10/20/us/angel-cloud-trnd/.
58. Charles Hunter, Frances Gardner Hunter, Roland Buck, *Angels on Assignment* (Hunter Books, 1979), 13.
59. Ibid.
60. Ibid., 11–16.
61. Ibid.
62. Ibid.
63. J. Rodman Williams, "Angels on Assignment," last accessed May 2, 2017, https://www.cbn.com/spirituallife/BibleStudyAndTheology/DrWilliams/ART_angels.pdf.
64. Ibid.
65. Charles Hunter, Frances Gardner Hunter, Roland Buck, *Angels on Assignment*, 45.
66. Ibid., 33.
67. https://www.cbn.com/spirituallife/BibleStudyAndTheology/DrWilliams/ART_angels.pdf
68. Ruth Ward Heflin, *Revival Glory* (Lulu Enterprises, 2013).
69. Rick Joyner, "Questions and Answers About the Present Outpouring," *MorningStar*, last accessed May 2, 2017, https://www.morningstarministries.org/resources/special-bulletins/2008/questions-and-answers-about-present-outpouring#.WP3jI1PyvjA.
70. J. Lee Grady, "Angels, Deception and a Cry for Biblical Truth," *CBN*, last accessed May 2, 2017, http://www1.cbn.com/biblestudy/angels%2C-deception-and-a-cry-for-biblical-truth.

71. Ibid.
72. "Mercy Is our New Currency," *Dutch Sheets Online*, last accessed May 2, 2017, https://dutchsheets.org/index.php/2016/12/21/mercy-is-our-new-currency/.
73. "Angelic Visitation, Vision, Healing," *Bethel*, last accessed May 2, 2017, http://www.ibethel.org/testimonies/angelic-visitation-vision-healing/.
74. Book found online in its entirety at the following: Che Ahn, *Say Goodbye to Powerless Christianity*, last accessed May 2, 2017, https://books.google.com/books?id=k7Mtfrp87bkC&pg=PT44&lpg=PT44&dq=che+ahn+hundreds+of+angels&source=bl&ots=giQufQrBs3&sig=D_42jndCny_Dsxznb_bfBWeydtw&hl=en&sa=X&ved=0ahUKEwiQldOm8NrSAhUEQiYKHaNEBKUQ6AEIIDAB#v=onepage&q=mott&f=false.
75. Ibid.
76. "Patricia King on Discerning Angels," YouTube video uploaded by Patricia King on November 14, 2016, last accessed May 2, 2017, https://www.youtube.com/watch?v=7DFd5AMxu4Y.
77. Jim Rawlins, "An Angelic Visitation Speaks to the Coming Awakening," May 10, 2015, *Charisma News*, last accessed May 2, 2017, http://www.charismanews.com/opinion/49560-an-angelic-visitation-speaks-to-the-coming-awakening.
78. Ibid.
79. Ibid.
80. "The Ministry of Angels," March 11, 2006, *Sid Roth Online*, last accessed May 2, 2017, http://sidroth.org/articles/ministry-angels/.
81. Tim Sheets, *Angel Armies: Releasing the Warriors of Heaven* (Destiny Image Publishers, Shippensburg, PA: 2016), 26–27.
82. Ibid.
83. "Timeline of Islam," *PBS*, last accessed May 2, 2017, http://www.pbs.org/wgbh/pages/frontline/teach/muslims/timeline.html.
84. "Islam," *Ecyclopaedia Britannica*, last accessed May 2, 2017, https://www.britannica.com/topic/Islam.
85. Ibid.

86. H. Donl Peterson, "Moroni—Joseph Smith's Tutor," January 1992, *The Church of Jesus Christ of Latter-Day Saints*, last accessed May 2, 2017, https://www.lds.org/ensign/1992/01/moroni-joseph-smiths-tutor?lang=eng.
87. "Chapter 9: The Atonement of Jesus Christ," from *Doctrines of the Gospel Student Manual* (2000), 22–26; accessed here May 2, 2017, https://www.lds.org/manual/doctrines-of-the-gospel-student-manual/chapter-9-the-atonement-of-jesus-christ?lang=eng.
88. "Worldwide Statistics," *Church of Jesus Christ of Latter-day Saints Newsroom*, last accessed May 2, 2017, http://www.mormonnewsroom.org/facts-and-statistics#.
89. John Zarrella and Patrick Oppman, "Pastor with 666 Tattoo Claims to Be Divine," February 19, 2007, *CNN News*, last accessed May 2, 2017, http://www.cnn.com/2007/US/02/16/miami.preacher/index.html?_s=PM:US.
90. Patricia King, *Dream Big* (Destiny Image Publishers, Shippensburg, PA: 2008), 61.
91. Mike Bickle, *Loving God: Daily Reflections for Intimacy with God* (Charisma House, Lake Mary, Florida: 2007), 291.
92. Tim Sheets, *Angel Armies*, 26–27.
93. For more information about Jeff Jansen and/or Global Fire Ministries, visit the website at: http://www.globalfireministries.com/.
94. Ibid.
95. James W. Goll, *Angelic Encounters: Engaging Help from Heaven* (Charisma House, Lake Mary, Florida: 2007). This book can be read in its entirety here: https://books.google.com/books?id=NEeQ35Trs-2AC&printsec=frontcover&dq=James+Goll,+author+of+Angelic+Encounters:+Engaging+Help+from+Heaven&hl=en&sa=X&ved=0ahUKEwim-YrNp9LTAhVN8GMKHbAJB20Q6AEIJjAA#v=onepage&q=James%20Goll%2C%20author%20of%20Angelic%20Encounters%3A%20Engaging%20Help%20from%20Heaven&f=false; last accessed May 2, 2017.
96. Ibid.

97. John Hutchinson, "What Is this Strange Sound from the Sky?" May 16, 2015, *Daily Mail*, last accessed May 2, 2017, http://www.dailymail.co.uk/travel/travel_news/article-3084260/What-strange-sound-sky-Noise-heard-globe-nearly-DECADE-explanation.html#ixzz4bh0U5p57.
98. Adam Eliyahu Berkowitz, "Mysterious Trumpet-Like Sounds Around World Leave Many In Hope of Messiah's Arrival," August 17, 2015, *Breaking Israel News*, last accessed May 2, 2017, https://www.breakingisraelnews.com/47020/mysterious-trumpet-sounds-world-leaves-manyhope-messiahs-arrival-jewish-world/.
99. George Harrison, "Terrifying Sound Heard throughout the World Is being Blamed on Donald Trump and Apparently Signals the Apocalypse," November 12, 2016, *The Sun*, last accessed May 2, 2017, https://www.thesun.co.uk/living/2170904/terrifying-sound-heard-throughout-the-world-is-being-blamed-on-donald-trump-and-apparently-signals-the-apocalypse/.
100. "End-times Expert Exposes 'Trumpets' in the Sky," May 30, 2015, last accessed May 2, 2017, http://www.wnd.com/2015/05/caution-urged-regarding-trumpets-in-the-sky/#bVfrYeru2Z8s7qUb.99.
101. Ibid.
102. "Signs of the Times: Angel of the Lord Appears in Arizona," YouTube video uploaded by Chaabar Yakal on January 16, 2017, last accessed May 2, 2017, https://www.youtube.com/watch?v=Q1SmoUErmkY.
103. "Ghost: Fourth Horseman of the Apocalypse MSNBC—Egyptian Riots Original Full Video," YouTube video uploaded by Fight0Tyranny on February 4, 2011, last accessed May 2, 2017, https://www.youtube.com/watch?v=gWQKOj9Sxkg.
104. "Green Horseman Appears in the Clouds Over Nottingham, UK," July 8, 2015, *UFO Sightings*, last accessed May 2, 2017, http://ufo-sightingshotspot.blogspot.com/2015/07/green-horseman-appears-in-clouds-over.html.
105. Joe Kovacs, "Sunrise 'Angel,' Cross in Sky Photographed Same Day!" January 1, 2015, *World Net Daily*, last

accessed May 2, 2017, http://www.wnd.com/2016/01/sunrise-angel-and-cross-photographed-same-day/.

106. "Massive Pentagram Forms in the Sky!! Prophetic Signs of the End Times!" December 22, 2013, *Before It's News*, last accessed May 2, 2017, http://beforeitsnews.com/paranormal/2013/12/massive-pentagram-forms-in-the-sky-prophetic-signs-of-the-end-times-video-2461864.html.
107. Tim Sheets, *Angel Armies*, 26–27.
108. "100 Most Frequently Asked Questions about the End Times," last accessed May 2, 2017, *Mike Bickle Online*, http://www.mikebickle.org.edgesuite.net/MikeBickleVOD/2008/100_Most_Frequently_Asked_Questions_about_the_End_Times.pdf.
109. Joe Kovacs, "Hand of God Sent Missile Into Sea," August 5, 2014, *World Net Daily*, last accessed May 2, 2017, http://www.wnd.com/2014/08/hand-of-god-sent-missile-into-sea/#YmMAJFxAXxy0OI0M.99.
110. Gordon Lindsay, *A Man Sent From God* (William Branham: 1950), 76–78.